D1037014

GRAPHIS EPHEMERA 1

GRAPHIS EPHEMERA 1

....

AN INTERNATIONAL COLLECTION OF PROMOTIONAL ART

GRAPHISCHE DOKUMENTE DES TÄGLICHEN LEBENS

LE GRAPHISME – UN ÉTAT D'ESPRIT AU QUOTIDIEN

EDITED BY·HERAUSGEGEBEN VON·EDITÉ PAR:

B. MARTIN PEDERSEN

PUBLISHER AND CREATIVE DIRECTOR: B. MARTIN PEDERSEN

EDITORS: HEINKE JENSSEN, ANNETTE CRANDALL

ASSISTANT EDITOR: JÖRG REIMANN

ART DIRECTORS: B. MARTIN PEDERSEN, RANDELL PEARSON

PHOTOGRAPHER: WALTER ZUBER

GRAPHIS PRESS CORP. ZÜRICH (SWITZERLAND)

(OPPOSITE) DESIGNER: POLLY CARPENTER, PHOTOGRAPHER: TERRY HEFFERNAN,
AGENCY: CARPENTER DESIGN, CLIENT: DEAN WITTER INTERNATIONAL, COUNTRY: USA

CONTENTS · INHALT · SOMMAIRE

REMARKS

WE EXTEND OUR HEARTFELT THANKS TO
CONTRIBUTORS THROUGHOUT THE WORLD
WHO HAVE MADE IT POSSIBLE TO PUBLISH A
WIDE AND INTERNATIONAL SPECTRUM OF
THE BEST WORK IN THIS FIELD.

ENTRY INSTRUCTIONS MAY BE REQUESTED AT:
GRAPHIS PRESS CORP.,
DUFOURSTRASSE 107,
8008 ZÜRICH, SWITZERLAND

ANMERKUNGEN

UNSER DANK GILT DEN EINSENDERN AUS
ALLER WELT, DIE ES UNS DURCH IHRE BEI-
TRÄGE ERMÖGLICHT HABEN, EIN BREITES,
INTERNATIONALES SPEKTRUM DER BESTEN
ARBEITEN ZU VERÖFFENTLICHEN.

TEILNAHMEBEDINGUNGEN:
GRAPHIS VERLAG AG,
DUFOURSTRASSE 107,
8008 ZÜRICH, SCHWEIZ

ANNOTATIONS

TOUTE NOTRE RECONNAISSANCE VA AUX
DESIGNERS DU MONDE ENTIER DONT LES
ENVOIS NOUS ONT PERMIS DE CONSTITUER
UN VASTE PANORAMA INTERNATIONAL DES
MEILLEURES CRÉATIONS.

MODALITÉS D'ENVOI DE TRAVAUX:
EDITIONS GRAPHIS,
DUFOURSTRASSE 107,
8008 ZÜRICH, SUISSE

(OPPOSITE) ART DIRECTOR: SUSAN CALDWELL DESIGNER: SUSAN CALDWELL AGENCY: THE Q DESIGN GROUP
CLIENT: NEW CANAAN SOCIETY FOR THE ARTS COUNTRY: USA

GRAPHIS PUBLICATIONS

GRAPHIS, THE INTERNATIONAL BI-MONTHLY JOURNAL OF VISUAL COMMUNICATION
GRAPHIS DESIGN, THE INTERNATIONAL ANNUAL OF DESIGN AND ILLUSTRATION
GRAPHIS ADVERTISING, THE INTERNATIONAL ANNUAL OF ADVERTISING
GRAPHIS BROCHURES, A COMPILATION OF BROCHURE DESIGN
GRAPHIS PHOTO, THE INTERNATIONAL ANNUAL OF PHOTOGRAPHY
GRAPHIS ALTERNATIVE PHOTOGRAPHY, THE INTERNATIONAL ANNUAL OF ALTERNATIVE PHOTOGRAPHY
GRAPHIS NUDES, A COLLECTION OF CAREFULLY SELECTED SOPHISTICATED IMAGES
GRAPHIS POSTER, THE INTERNATIONAL ANNUAL OF POSTER ART
GRAPHIS PACKAGING, AN INTERNATIONAL COMPILATION OF PACKAGING DESIGN
GRAPHIS LETTERHEAD, AN INTERNATIONAL COMPILATION OF LETTERHEAD DESIGN
GRAPHIS DIAGRAM, THE GRAPHIC VISUALIZATION OF ABSTRACT, TECHNICAL AND STATISTICAL FACTS AND FUNCTIONS
GRAPHIS LOGO, AN INTERNATIONAL COMPILATION OF LOGOS
GRAPHIS EPHEMERA, AN INTERNATIONAL COLLECTION OF PROMOTIONAL ART
GRAPHIS PUBLICATION, AN INTERNATIONAL SURVEY OF THE BEST IN MAGAZINE DESIGN
GRAPHIS ANNUAL REPORTS, AN INTERNATIONAL COMPILATION OF THE BEST DESIGNED ANNUAL REPORTS
GRAPHIS CORPORATE IDENTITY, AN INTERNATIONAL COMPILATION OF THE BEST IN CORPORATE IDENTITY DESIGN
GRAPHIS TYPOGRAPHY, AN INTERNATIONAL COMPILATION OF THE BEST IN TYPOGRAPHIC DESIGN
ART FOR SURVIVAL: THE ILLUSTRATOR AND THE ENVIRONMENT, A DOCUMENT OF ART IN THE SERVICE OF MAN.
THE GRAPHIC DESIGNER'S GREEN BOOK, ENVIRONMENTAL RESOURCES FOR THE DESIGN AND PRINT INDUSTRIES

GRAPHIS PUBLIKATIONEN

GRAPHIS, DIE INTERNATIONALE ZWEIMONATSZEITSCHRIFT DER VISUELLEN KOMMUNIKATION
GRAPHIS DESIGN, DAS INTERNATIONALE JAHRBUCH ÜBER DESIGN UND ILLUSTRATION
GRAPHIS ADVERTISING, DAS INTERNATIONALE JAHRBUCH DER WERBUNG
GRAPHIS BROCHURES, BROSCHÜRENDESIGN IM INTERNATIONAL ÜBERBLICK
GRAPHIS PHOTO, DAS INTERNATIONALE JAHRBUCH DER PHOTOGRAPHIE
GRAPHIS ALTERNATIVE PHOTOGRAPHY, DAS INTERNATIONALE JAHRBUCH ÜBER ALTERNATIVE PHOTOGRAPHIE
GRAPHIS NUDES, EINE SAMMLUNG SORGFÄLTIG AUSGEWÄHLTER AKTPHOTOGRAPHIE
GRAPHIS POSTER, DAS INTERNATIONALE JAHRBUCH DER PLAKATKUNST
GRAPHIS PACKAGING, EIN INTERNATIONALER ÜBERBLICK ÜBER DIE PACKUNGSGESTALTUNG
GRAPHIS LETTERHEAD, EIN INTERNATIONALER ÜBERBLICK ÜBER BRIEFPAPIERGESTALTUNG
GRAPHIS DIAGRAM, DIE GRAPHISCHE DARSTELLUNG ABSTRAKTER TECHNISCHER UND STATISTISCHER DATEN UND FAKTEN
GRAPHIS LOGO, EINE INTERNATIONALE AUSWAHL VON FIRMEN-LOGOS
GRAPHIS EPHEMERA, EINE INTERNATIONALE SAMMLUNG GRAPHISCHER DOKUMENTE DES TÄGLICHEN LEBENS
GRAPHIS MAGAZINDESIGN, EINE INTERNATIONALE ZUSAMMENSTELLUNG DES BESTEN ZEITSCHRIFTEN-DESIGNS
GRAPHIS ANNUAL REPORTS, EIN INTERNATIONALER ÜBERBLICK ÜBER DIE GESTALTUNG VON JAHRESBERICHTEN
GRAPHIS CORPORATE IDENTITY, EINE INTERNATIONALE AUSWAHL DES BESTEN CORPORATE IDENTITY DESIGNS
GRAPHIS TYPOGRAPHY, EINE INTERNATIONALE ZUSAMMENSTELLUNG DES BESTEN TYPOGRAPHIE DESIGN
ART FOR SURVIVAL: THE ILLUSTRATOR AND THE ENVIRONMENT, EIN DOKUMENT ÜBER DIE KUNST IM DIENSTE DES MENSCHEN
THE GRAPHIC DESIGNER'S GREEN BOOK, UMWELTKONZEPTE DER DESIGN- UND DRUCKINDUSTRIE

PUBLICATIONS GRAPHIS

GRAPHIS, LA REVUE BIMESTRIELLE INTERNATIONALE DE LA COMMUNICATION VISUELLE
GRAPHIS DESIGN, LE RÉPERTOIRE INTERNATIONAL DE LA COMMUNICATION VISUELLE
GRAPHIS ADVERTISING, LE RÉPERTOIRE INTERNATIONAL DE LA PUBLICITÉ
GRAPHIS BROCHURES, UNE COMPILATION INTERNATIONALE SUR LE DESIGN DES BROCHURES
GRAPHIS PHOTO, LE RÉPERTOIRE INTERNATIONAL DE LA PHOTOGRAPHIE
GRAPHIS ALTERNATIVE PHOTOGRAPHY, LE RÉPERTOIRE INTERNATIONAL DE LA PHOTOGRAPHIE ALTERNATIVE
GRAPHIS NUDES, UN FLORILÈGE DE LA PHOTOGRAPHIE DE NUS
GRAPHIS POSTER, LE RÉPERTOIRE INTERNATIONAL DE L'AFFICHE
GRAPHIS PACKAGING, LE RÉPERTOIRE INTERNATIONAL DE LA CRÉATION D'EMBALLAGES
GRAPHIS LETTERHEAD, LE RÉPERTOIRE INTERNATIONAL DU DESIGN DE PAPIER À LETTRES
GRAPHIS DIAGRAM, LE RÉPERTOIRE GRAPHIQUE DE FAITS ET DONNÉES ABSTRAITS, TECHNIQUES ET STATISTIQUES
GRAPHIS LOGO, LE RÉPERTOIRE INTERNATIONAL DU LOGO
GRAPHIS EPHEMERA, LE GRAPHISME – UN ÉTAT D'ESPRIT AU QUOTIDIEN
GRAPHIS PUBLICATION, LE RÉPERTOIRE INTERNATIONAL DU DESIGN DE PÉRIODIQUES
GRAPHIS ANNUAL REPORTS, PANORAMA INTERNATIONAL DU MEILLEUR DESIGN DE RAPPORTS ANNUELS D'ENTREPRISES
GRAPHIS CORPORATE IDENTITY, PANORAMA INTERNATIONAL DU MEILLEUR DESIGN D'IDENTITÉ CORPORATE
GRAPHIS TYPOGRAPHY, LE RÉPERTOIRE INTERNATIONAL DU MEILLEUR DESIGN DE TYPOGRAPHIE
ART FOR SURVIVAL: THE ILLUSTRATOR AND THE ENVIRONMENT, L'ART AU SERVICE DE LA SURVIE
THE GRAPHIC DESIGNER'S GREEN BOOK, L'ÉCOLOGIE APPLIQUÉE AU DESIGN ET À L'INDUSTRIE GRAPHIQUE

PUBLICATION NO. 241 (ISBN 3–85709–456–7)
© COPYRIGHT UNDER UNIVERSAL COPYRIGHT CONVENTION
COPYRIGHT © 1995 BY GRAPHIS PRESS CORP., DUFOURSTRASSE 107, 8008 ZURICH, SWITZERLAND
JACKET AND BOOK DESIGN COPYRIGHT © 1995 BY PEDERSEN DESIGN
141 LEXINGTON AVENUE, NEW YORK, N.Y. 10016 USA

PRINTED IN JAPAN BY TOPPAN PRINTING CO., LTD.

COMMENTARIES

KOMMENTARE

COMMENTAIRES

In December 1843, a young British civil servant, too busy to write letters of Christmas greeting to all his friends, commissioned the first Christmas card. According to legend, Henry Cole, who later became the first Director of the Victoria and Albert Museum, thus initiated a custom that now supports a multi-million dollar international business. □ Cole could certainly be forgiven for his failure to conduct lengthy correspondence. As well as writing children's books, he was closely involved with the development of the railways, the organization of government design schools, and the conception of his special "child," the South Kensington Museum (later the V&A). Another of his favorite causes, the Penny Post, ensured the success of his new Christmas card trend. Introduced in 1840, it enabled large sections of the population to communicate by mail. The opportunity was enthusiastically embraced during the festive season when distant friends and far-flung families made annual contact with each other. □ In our contemporary mobile society, families and friends are often separated by huge distances, but even in an era of faxes and E-mail, the sending of Christmas cards remains as popular as ever. As the 1993 exhibition at the V&A indicated, changes in the design and style of cards have been gradual and the majority of cards sent today are

JAN BURNEY IS A FREELANCE WRITER ON ARCHITECTURE AND DESIGN, BASED IN LONDON. EDUCATED AT THE UNIVERSITIES OF EDINBURGH AND SUSSEX, SHE WAS EDITOR OF *DESIGNER* MAGAZINE. SHE IS A FREQUENT CONTRIBUTOR TO *GRAPHIS* AND OTHER EUROPEAN AND AMERICAN MAGAZINES. HER MOST RECENT BOOK IS *ETTORE SOTTSASS DESIGN HERO* (HARPERCOLLINS, 1993).

not radically different, in visual spirit, from the cards dispatched by Cole in 1843. □ Cole's card was illustrated by the painter John Callcott Horsley, and his composition was inspired by the form of a church altarpiece. Within a framework of tree branches and vines, the central image of family festivity is flanked by illustrations of charitable largesse. These twin themes of merry-making and charity remained a persistent feature of Christmas cards through the Victorian period. □ Cole's card was published by his own lithography company in a hand-colored edition of one thousand and sold to the public for one shilling per card, then the price of dinner in a good restaurant. By 1850, however, the cost of cards had come down and the demand for cards provided good business for several publishing companies. By the end of the 19th century, sentimental scenes of robins, yule logs, and sleigh rides in the snow were joined by images of Father Christmas and religious illustrations. More sophisticated cards were influenced by the fashion for Japanese style and comic imagery was even beginning to creep in. □ Christmas cards remained a British phenomenon until 1874, when the American publisher Louis Prang recognized their commerical potential and began producing cards at his company in Boston. He introduced an elongat-

ed format and black background to emphasize the other bright colors and offered high monetary prizes for the winning designs in the competitions he organized. □ By the beginning of the 20th century, Christmas card production had become a highly profitable business, although in recent years a high proportion of consumers have been choosing to send cards with the proceeds going to charity. Many cards are now also printed on recycled paper. In terms of style, the kitsch conventions of traditional cards have been challenged by fine art and cartoon imagery. Illustration for, and sometimes by, children is also popular. Arthur Rackham and Beatrix Potter are among the many illustrators who have created designs for Christmas cards. □ The custom of sending cards at Christmas continues to flourish in a multi-media age. Cole would undoubtedly be delighted that the tradition he established in 1848 now provides a form of patronage for artists of all descriptions. □ The Victoria and Albert Museum at South Kensington, London SW7 2RL is open Tuesday through Sunday from 9.00 a.m. to 5.50 p.m., and Mondays from 12.00 to 5.50 p.m. Many of the cards on display in the exhibition were taken from the George Buday collection comprising over ten thousand cards, which he left to the museum after his death. ■

Im Dezember 1843 gab ein junger britischer Staatsbeamter, der keine Zeit hatte, all seinen Freunden zu Weihnachten Briefe zu schreiben, die erste Weihnachtskarte in Auftrag. Er hiess Henry Cole und sollte später der erste Direktor des Victoria and Albert Museum werden. Nach der Überlieferung war er es, der mit seinem Auftrag einen Brauch ins Leben rief, der inzwischen zum Gegenstand eines internationalen Multimillionen-Dollar-Geschäfts geworden ist. □ Man kann Cole kaum übelnehmen, dass er keine Zeit für ausgedehnte Briefwechsel fand. Er schrieb nicht nur Kinderbücher, sondern war auch in die Entwicklung des Schienenverkehrs involviert, in den Aufbau staatlicher Designschulen, und er arbeitete am Konzept seines «Lieblingskindes», des South Kensington Museum (später V&A). Ein anderes Lieblingsprojekt von ihm, die «Penny Post», verhalf dem neuen Weihnachtskartenbrauch zum Durchbruch. Diese Post wurde 1840 eingeführt und ermöglichte grossen Teilen der Bevölkerung, per Post zu kommunizieren, und von dieser Gelegenheit wurde vor allem während der Weihnachtszeit begeistert Gebrauch gemacht, um einmal jährlich Kontakt mit Freunden in der Ferne oder mit weit verstreuten Verwandten aufzunehmen. □ In unserer mobilen Gesellschaft sind Familien und Freunde oft durch riesige Distanzen getrennt, und trotz Fax und E-Mail ist das Versenden von Weihnachtskarten so beliebt wie je zuvor. Eine Ausstellung im V&A Museum 1993 war der Weihnachtskarte gewidmet, und hier konnte man feststellen, wie sich Gestaltung und Stil der Karten nur ganz allmählich verändert haben. Die Mehrzahl der heutigen Karten ist in ihrer visuellen Botschaft gar nicht so weit entfernt von den Karten, die Cole 1843 verschickte. □ Coles Karte war von dem Illustrator und Maler John Callcott Horsley illustriert, und

seine Komposition war von der Form eines Kirchenaltarbildes inspiriert. Umrahmt von Ästen und Reben wird das zentrale Motiv des Familienfestes von Illustrationen wohltätiger Grosszügigkeit begleitet. Diese Kombination von Fröhlichkeit und Wohltätigkeit blieb während der ganzen Viktorianischen Epoche ein fortwährendes Thema. □ Coles Karte wurde von seiner eigenen Lithographenanstalt in einer handkolorierten Auflage von 1000 Stück herausgegeben und für einen Shilling pro Karte verkauft, ein Betrag, den man damals für ein Abendessen in einem guten Restaurant bezahlte. Bereits 1850 jedoch war der Preis für die Karten auf einem annehmbaren Niveau, und die Nachfrage wurde für viele Verlage ein gutes Geschäft. Gegen Ende des 19. Jahrhunderts fand man ausser den sentimentalen Illustrationen von Rotkehlchen, geschmückten Tannen und Schlittenfahrten im Schnee auch Bilder des Weihnachtsmanns und religiöse Darstellungen. Anspruchsvollere Karten waren von der Begeisterung für den japanischen Still beeinflusst, und sogar der Comicstil schlich sich ein. □ Bis 1874 blieben Weihnachtskarten ein britisches Phänomen, dann erkannte der amerikanische Verleger Louis Prang ihr kommerzielles Potential, und er begann, in seiner Firma in Boston Karten zu produzieren. Er führte das längliche Format ein und den schwarzen Hintergrund, der die anderen Farben leuchten liess, und er organisierte Wettbewerbe für die Gestaltung und Illustration von Weihnachtskarten, deren Gewinner mit ansehnlichen Geldpreisen ausgezeichnet wurden. □ Zu Beginn des 20. Jahrhunderts war die Weihnachtskartenherstellung bereits ein äusserst einträgliches Geschäft, obwohl viele Verbraucher in den letzten Jahren dazu übergegangen sind, Karten zu kaufen, deren Erlös für wohltätige Zwecke verwendet wird. Viele Karten sind

JAN BURNEY LEBT ALS FREIE JOURNALISTIN IN LONDON. IHRE FACHGEBIETE SIND ARCHITEKTUR UND DESIGN. SIE SCHREIBT REGELMÄSSIG FÜR GRAPHIS UND ANDERE EUROPÄISCHE UND AMERIKANISCHE ZEITSCHRIFTEN UND WAR REDAKTEURIN DES MAGAZINS DESIGNER. IHR NEUSTES BUCH «ETTORE SOTTSASS: DESIGN HERO» IST 1993 ALS PAPERBACK BEI HARPERCOLLINS ERSCHIENEN.

Compliments of the season.

heute auf wiederverwertetes Papier gedruckt. Was den Stil angeht, so machen heute Kunst- und Comics den eher kitschigen Motiven der konventionellen Karten Konkurrenz. Illustrationen für Kinder – und manchmal von ihnen – sind ebenfalls sehr beliebt. Arthur Rackham und Beatrix Potter behören zu den vielen Illustratoren, die Entwürfe für Weihnachtskarten gemacht haben. □ Der Brauch, Weihnachtskarten zu verschicken, floriert nach wie vor, auch im Multimedia-Zeitalter.

Cole wäre zweifellos glücklich festzustellen, dass die von ihm 1848 ins Leben gerufene Tradition eine Form der Unterstützung für Künstler aller Art bedeutet. □ Das Victoria & Albert Museum, South Kensington, London SW7 2RL ist von Dienstag bis Sonntag zwischen 9.00 und 17.50 Uhr geöffnet, Montags von 12.00–17.50 Uhr. Ein grosser Teil der Ausstellung im V&A stammte aus der Sammlung des Museums – über 10 000 Karten aus dem Nachlass des Sammlers George Buday. ■

En décembre 1843, un jeune fonctionnaire britannique, qui ne trouvait pas le temps d'écrire des lettres pour adresser ses vœux de Noël à l'ensemble de ses amis, fit réaliser ce qui devait constituer la première carte de Noël. La légende veut que ce même Henry Cole, qui devint plus tard le premier conservateur du Victoria and Albert Museum, fut ainsi l'instigateur d'une coutume qui génère aujourd'hui un volume d'affaires de plusieurs millions de dollars. □ On pourra sans doute facilement pardonner à Mr. Cole de ne pas avoir voulu assumer une correspondance trop volumineuse. Tout en écrivant des livres pour enfants, il participa activement au développement des chemins de fer et à la mise en place des premières écoles publiques d'arts décoratifs sans oublier la conception de cet «enfant» très spécial qui fut le sien, à savoir le South Kensington Museum (qui devait devenir ensuite le Victoria and Albert Museum). C'est également l'une des causes auxquelles il s'est dévoué – le système de la «poste à deux sous» – qui a permis à la nouvelle tendance des cartes de Noël de rencontrer un franc succès. Instauré en 1840, ce système offrit au plus grand nombre la possibilité de communiquer par courrier et, durant la période des fêtes, cette nouvelle opportunité fut accueillie avec beaucoup d'enthousiasme par les amis que la distance séparait et les familles éparpillées qui purent ainsi reprendre contact chaque année. □ Aujourd'hui, au sein de notre société vouée à la mobilité, les familles et les amis sont souvent séparés par de très longues distances et malgré les communications par télécopie ou par courrier électronique, l'envoi de cartes de voeux demeure une coutume très largement pratiquée. Comme en a témoigné l'exposition de 1993 tenue au Victoria and Albert Museum, les changements de style et de conception des cartes de voeux ont été très progressifs et la plupart des cartes expédiées aujourd'hui ne sont pas radicalement différentes, dans leur inspiration visuelle, de celles qu'a pu adresser Mr. Cole en 1843. □ La carte de Cole avait été illustrée par le peintre John Callcott Horsley dont la composition puisait son inspiration dans la forme du retable d'une église. Encadrée par un décor de branches d'arbre et de vignes, l'image centrale de la fête de famille côtoyait des représentations évoquant l'abondance et la générosité. Ce double thème de la réjouissance et de la charité est resté la caractéristique prédominante des cartes de Noël durant toute l'époque victorienne. □ La carte de Cole a été publiée par sa propre entreprise de lithographie

en mille exemplaires peints à la main puis proposée au public au prix de un shilling la carte, ce qui, à l'époque, était le prix d'un dîner dans un bon restaurant. Toutefois, dès 1850, le prix des cartes régressa à un niveau beaucoup plus raisonnable et la demande croissante du public permit à plusieurs sociétés d'édition de connaître un excellent développement. A la fin du 19ème siècle, les images sentimentales de rouge-gorge, de bûches de Noël et de traîneaux sur fond de neige furent complétées par des représentations du Père-Noël et des scènes religieuses tandis que des cartes plus sophistiquées, influencées par le style japonais, mais aussi les premières représentations humoristiques firent leur apparition. □ Les cartes de Noël demeurèrent un phénomène typiquement britannique jusqu'en 1874. C'est alors qu'un éditeur américain du nom de Louis Prang prit conscience de leur potentiel commercial et lança une production de cartes dans son entreprise de Boston. □ Il introduisit un nouveau format allongé ainsi qu'un fond noir destiné à mettre en valeur les autres couleurs vives utilisées et organisa des concours de dessin avec attribution de prix d'un montant alléchant aux vainqueurs. □ Dès le début du vingtième siècle, la production des cartes de Noël est devenue une activité extrêmement lucrative. On note toutefois qu'au cours de ces dernières années, les consommateurs ont opté pour des cartes avec attribution des recettes des ventes à des organismes de charité. De même, nombre de cartes sont aujourd'hui imprimées sur du papier recyclé. En matière de graphisme, le style très kitsch des cartes traditionnelles a été quelque peu battu en brèche par les illustrations artistiques et les dessins humoristiques. Les dessins pour enfants, et parfois même réalisés par des enfants, ont aussi gagné en popularité. Arthur Rackham et Beatrix Potter font partie des nombreux créateurs spécialisés dans les illustrations pour cartes de Noël. □ A l'heure de la communication multimédia, la tradition de la carte de Noël est toujours aussi vivante. Cole serait très certainement ravi de constater que cette coutume instaurée en 1843 équivaut aujourd'hui à une forme de mécénat pour bon nombre d'artistes aux tendances les plus variées. □ Le musée Victoria and Albert de South Kensington à Londres est ouvert du mardi au dimanche de 9.00 à 17.50 heures et le lundi de 12.00 à 17.50. Une grande partie de l'exposition de cartes de Noël du V&A provient de la collection particulière du musée qui comporte un fonds de plus de 10 000 cartes du collectionneur George Buday. ■

JAN BURNEY TRAVAILLE COMME JOURNALISTE LIBRE À LONDRES. DES DOMAINES DE PRÉDILECTION SONT L'ARCHITECTURE ET LE DESIGN. ELLE PUBLIE RÉGULIÈREMENT DES ARTICLES DANS LE MAGAZINE GRAPHIS AINSI QUE DANS D'AUTRE REVEUS EN EUROPE ET AUX ETATS-UNIS. SON DERNIER OUVRAGE INTITULÉ «ETTORE SOTTSASS: DESIGN HERO» EST PARUE EN 1993 CHEZ HARPERCOLLINS.

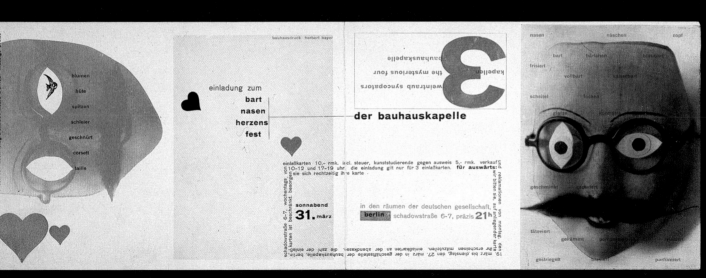

HERBERT BAYER: INVITATION TO A BAUHAUS PARTY, 1928. ORIGINAL IN THE BAUHAUS ARCHIVES. PHOTO BY ATERLIER SCHNEIDER, BERLIN.

Although seldom shown to juries or published in annuals, and only by exception found in artists' portfolios and monographs, these small and often delightful works of art fulfill the communicative function from which the entire branch lives. Ephemera! A collective name for all of those varied and fleeting trivialities that cannot really be considered a commission, but which must be completed nevertheless. Occasions—studio openings, movings, marriages, birth announcements—are as justifiable as the common greeting cards (New Year's, Easter, birthdays, Christmas). □ Whoever earns his living in the realization of creative ideas cannot avoid ephemera. Indeed, the real artist is ambitious enough to deal with such minor matters alone, resolving them in the spirit of Kurt Tucholsky who admitted that "my modest need for prose I write myself." Indeed, ephemera often reflect very personal matters that are only meant for a circle of good friends and valued acquaintances. □ Thus begins a Sisyphean task, which bears no relation to the size of the finished greeting—if it is to be finished at all! There are enough examples of occasions where great opportunities were missed—the marriage gone astray, the newborn now in school, the creative team disbanded. (No, dear reader, I am not really alluding to you in particular!) □ Once captured by

HERBERT LECHNER WAS EDITOR-IN-CHIEF OF THE TRADE MAGAZINE *GRAPHIK VISUELLES MARKETING* FOR FIVE YEARS. SINCE 1986, HE HAS WORKED AS A FREELANCE JOURNALIST IN MUNICH, FREQUENTLY WRITING ABOUT "VISUAL CULTURE." HE IS A PARTNER IN BASSE & LECHNER, A SMALL PUBLISHING FIRM SPECIALIZING IN LIMITED EDITIONS. HE IS THE AUTHOR OF SEVERAL BOOKS, INCLUDING *THE HISTORY OF MODERN TYPOGRAPHY* AND *CARTOONS AND CARICATURES IN ADVERTISING.*

the challenge of self-expression in small format, the artist begins a game of roulette, tossing between designing and discarding, a game that can rapidly become a mania. If client and designer are one and the same, then the designer suddenly starts to appreciate his own clients again, because another person is seldom as critical as one is of oneself. Somehow it seems so easy—like jumping through a burning hoop while balancing on a tightrope, snarling lions and spectators waiting below. Still, the skill of the artist is also in smiling, and in making everything appear quite easy. □ How fortunate that the painful birth of the finished card is not revealed. ("Ah that one, that was a quick sketch..." can only be heard in the late hours amongst trusted friends. And then these colleagues, shaken by similar problems, nod knowingly: "Of course.") □ Like diamonds (which are known to grow only under enormous pressure), the diminutive form of these truly precious objects emerges from the creative process. The wealth of ideas invested is breathtaking. There is hardly a technique, hardly a material, hardly a gag missing from this struggle for a "small" resolution to a problem. Postcards of Plexiglas and hand-finished wooden boxes, printed

silk scarves and books in miniature. To paraphrase Goethe, "the master reveals himself in limitation." Did our classical writers also set down texts for Christmas cards? How skillfully the seemingly limited possibilities are played out. □ But in this case, a little can also mean a great deal. Alone the simple card, which is offered here in its manifold variations is remembered as distinct, amusing, and evocative. Does the direct marketer ever receive such praise? □ The old standby, paper, is still the preferred material for every kind of ephemeron. Through folding and twisting, punching and pleating, not only the designer's inclination to play is satisfied, but that of the recipient as well. Origami is wisely considered an art form by the Japanese. □ The recipient is pleased, smiles, keeps the card for a while, perhaps contemplates it once more, and then it disappears as new and other small sensations claim his attention. Nevertheless, are these endearing and passing gems not worth all our effort and commitment? To paraphrase Schiller: "Man plays only there where he is a human being in the full sense of the word, and he is only a complete human being in the place where he plays." (He did indeed write texts for Christmas cards!) ∎

Ganz selten tauchen sie einmal bei Jurierungen und in Jahrbüchern auf, auch in den Mappen und Monographien der Künstler sind sie nur in Ausnahmen zu finden. Und das, obwohl sie in vielen Fällen kleine, bezaubernde Kunstwerke sind und ausserdem die kommunikative Aufgabe, von der die gesamte Branche lebt, am reinsten erfüllen: Ephemera! Sammelbegriff für all' jene buntgemischten und schnell vergänglichen Nebensächlichkeiten, die eigentlich keinen Auftrag darstellen, aber eben doch verfertigt werden müssen. Anlässe gibt es in Hülle und Fülle – Ateliereröffnung, Umzug, Geburtsanzeigen und immer wieder Glückwunschkarten (Neujahr, Weihnachten, Ostern, Geburtstage und die Reaktionen auf die Ephemera der lieben Kollegen). □ Wer sein Geld mit gestalterischen Ideen und ihrer Umsetzung verdient, der entkommt ihnen nicht, denn natürlich legt man seinen Ehrgeiz darein, solche Kleinigkeiten eben mal selbst zu erledigen, ganz im Sinne von Kurt Tucholsky: «Ich schreibe mir meinen kleinen Bedarf an Prosa lieber selber». Ausserdem sind es ja ganz persönliche Anliegen, die hier einem Kreis guter Freunde, lieber Bekannter, wichtiger Kontakte vermittelt werden sollen, wem sollte man die schon überlassen? □ Doch damit beginnt eine Sisyphusarbeit, die in keinem Verhältnis zur Grösse des fertigen Grusses steht. Wenn er denn fertig wird! Es gibt Beispiele, da ist der Anlass passé – die Ehe auseinander, das Neugeborene schulpflichtig, die Studio-Gemeinschaft zerbrochen –, bevor noch der grosse Wurf gelungen ist. (Nein, nein, verehrter Leser, ich habe wirklich nicht auf Sie speziell angespielt.) □ Ephemer sind diese Objekte nämlich zumeist nur für den Empfänger. Für den Kreativen, einmal gepackt von der Herausforderung der Selbstdarstellung im Kleinformat, beginnt ein Roulettespiel zwischen Entwerfen und Verwerfen,

das schnell zur Manie werden kann. Sind Auftraggeber und Ausführender identisch, dann lernt man plötzlich wieder seine Kunden schätzen. Denn so kritisch – im ganzen Doppelsinn des Wortes – wie man selbst, ist wohl kein anderer. Dabei scheint es doch so einfach – etwa so, wie auf dem Hochseil durch einen brennenden Reifen zu springen, während unten zähnefletschende Löwen und Zuschauer warten. Die Kunst des Artisten besteht eben auch darin, zu lächeln und alles ganz leicht wirken zu lassen. □ Welch ein Glück, dass niemand dem fertigen Kärtchen diese Geburtswehen mehr ansieht. (Nur im ganz vertrauten Kollegenkreis hört man zu fortgeschrittener Stunde mal ein «Ach, das, das hab ich schnell so hinskizziert». Und die Kollegen, von ähnlichen Problemen geschüttelt, nicken wissend: «Genau».) □ Dabei lässt die kleine Form wahre Pretiosen der kreativen Szene entstehen, sozusagen Diamanten (die bekanntlich auch nur unter immensem Druck wachsen!) Der investierte Einfallsreichtum ist atemberaubend. Kaum eine Technik, kaum ein Material, kaum ein Gag fehlt beim Ringen um die kleine Lösung. Postkarten aus Plexiglas und handgefertigte Holzkistchen sind ebenso zu finden wie bedruckte T-Shirts und Kleinstbücher. In der Beschränkung zeigt sich erst der Meister – haben unsere Klassiker eigentlich auch Weihnachtskarten getextet? –, denn wie gekonnt wird hier mit den scheinbar knappen Möglichkeiten gespielt. □ Aber auch wenig ist da schon sehr viel: Allein die schlichte Karte, welche Variationsbreite wird hier aufgeboten, um unverwechselbar, witzig und eindrucksvoll in Erinnerung zu bleiben. Bekommen eigentlich die Direkt Marketer nie solche Grüsse? □ Wie geduldig das gute alte Papier ist – nach wie vor der liebste Grundstoff für Ephemera jeder Art –, das erweist sich aber erst, wenn noch eine Dimension

HERBERT LECHNER WAR FÜNF JAHRE CHEFREDAKTEUR DER FACHZEITSCHRIFT GRAPHIK VISUELLES MARKETING. ER ARBEITET HEUTE ALS FREIER AUTOR UND TEXTER IN MÜNCHEN. ER HAT VERSCHIEDENE BÜCHER VERÖFFENTLICHT, UNTER ANDEREM ÜBER «DIE GESCHICHTE DER MODERNEN TYPOGRAPHIE» UND ÜBER «CARTOONS UND KARIKATUR IN DER WERBUNG».

dazukommt: Mit Falten und Falzen, Stanzen und Staunen wird nicht nur der eigene Spieltrieb, sondern auch der des Empfängers befriedigt – ein entscheidender Gesichtspunkt. Nicht umsonst gilt Origami bei den weisen Japanern als Kunstform. Manche dieser filigranen Kunstwerke offenbaren allerdings schon in ihrer Zerbrechlichkeit, dass Ephemera halt nicht für die Ewigkeit gemacht sind. □ Der Empfänger freut sich, schmunzelt, hebt das Kärtchen eine Weile auf, zeigt es vielleicht sogar noch einmal her – doch dann ist es verschwunden, und neue, kleine Sensationen verlangen seine Aufmerksamkeit. Und trotzdem: Sind diese liebenswerten, vergänglichen Kostbarkeiten nicht all unserer Mühen und unseres Engagements wert? Denn, so Schiller: «Der Mensch spielt nur, wo er in voller Bedeutung des Wortes Mensch ist, und er ist nur da ganz Mensch, wo er spielt.» (Also hat er doch Weihnachtskarten getextet!) ∎

....

Il est plutôt rare de les voir dans des compilations annuelles ou soumises à l'appréciation des jurés; dans les monographies et les cartons à dessin des artistes, elles ne sont pas non plus légion. Souvent, elles n'en sont pas moins de petits chefs-d'œuvre exquis qui remplissent au mieux les tâches de communication dont vit une branche tout entière: Ephemera! Tel est le terme générique désignant toutes ces créations secondaires, aussi variées qu'éphémères, qui ne représentent pas un contrat en soi, mais nécessitent cependant un travail de conception. Et ce ne sont pas les occasions qui manquent : inauguration d'un atelier, déménagement, mariage, faire-part de naissance et, encore et toujours, les cartes de vœux (Nouvel-An, Pâques, les anniversaires, Noël). □ Quiconque gagne sa vie grâce à son génie créatif, à ses idées et à leur réalisation n'y échappe pas. En effet, on n'est pas peu fier de réaliser soi-même ce genre de «bricole» lorsque l'occasion se présente. Kurt Tucholsky abondait d'ailleurs dans ce sens: «Je préfère rédiger moi-même le peu de prose dont j'ai besoin.» En outre, il s'agit de messages strictement personnels que l'on transmet à des amis intimes, à des connaissances ou à des relations importantes. Pourquoi donc s'en remettre à quelqu'un d'autre ? □ Mais c'est là que commence un véritable travail de Titan qui n'a aucun rapport avec l'œuvre parachevée – si ce stade devait être atteint un jour! Parfois, avant même d'avoir réussi un coup de maître, l'occasion appartient déjà au passé – les heureux mariés sont au chapitre du divorce, le nouveau-né est en âge de scolarité et les cohabitants du studio ne cohabitent plus. (Détrompez-vous, cher lecteur, ce n'est pas à vous en particulier que je m'adressais.) □ Éphémères, ces objets ne le sont en général que pour le destinataire. Pour le créatif, c'est une autre paire de manches. Une fois qu'il s'est laissé emballer par le défi de faire sa propre mise en scène en version petit format, commence alors un vrai casse-tête chinois entre ébauche et rejet, une opération qui peut se répéter maintes fois jusqu'à l'obsession. Si le mandant se trouve être également l'exécutant, on en vient tout à coup à apprécier ses clients. On n'est jamais aussi critique qu'envers soi-même, n'est-ce pas? Et pourtant, cela paraît si simple, comme de sauter à travers un cerceau en feu, tel un funambule, pendant que plus bas, à ses pieds, une horde de lions, tous crocs dehors, et les spectateurs attendent... Or, tout l'art de l'artiste consiste aussi à sourire, à donner l'impression que, oui, finalement c'est un jeu d'enfant. □ Quelle chance que personne n'assiste aux douleurs, aux contractions qui accompagnent la naissance de la petite carte. (Seuls quelques bons collègues au parfum ont l'occasion d'entendre, une fois que l'heure de la délivrance approche, «Oh, ce n'est rien de fracassant, j'ai juste fait une esquisse, comme ça.» Et ces mêmes collègues, tracassés par les mêmes problèmes, opinent du chef, en toute connaissance de cause: «Mais oui, c'est ça.») □ Toujours est-il que ces petits formats se transforment en objets précieux, en diamants pour ainsi dire (qui ne voient le jour, comme chacun sait, que sous une pression énorme!). Mais que de trouvailles! De quoi rester pantois. Aucune technique, aucun matériau, aucune astuce n'a été ignorée dans cette lutte acharnée pour vaincre, trouver la «mini-solution». Cartes postales en plexiglas, petites boîtes en bois réalisées à la main, carrés de soie imprimés, livres miniature, tout y est. «C'est dans l'indigence que l'on reconnaît le vrai maître» – les auteurs clasiques allemands ont-ils eux aussi rédigé des cartes de vœux pour Noël? –, car avec quelle maestria on s'est adonnés au jeu, avec des moyens apparemment limités. D'un petit rien naissent des merveilles: une carte toute simple se décline ici à l'infini, changements de format ou de tout autre paramètre, pour rester gravée dans la mémoire, faire sourire, devenir unique. En admirant ces petits chefs-d'œuvre, on peut se demander si les ténors du marketing direct reçoivent de temps à autre de tels messages? □ Pour découvrir les trésors de patience que recèle ce bon vieux papier – numéro un incontesté en matière d'annonces ou de faire-part, toutes catégories confondues –, il faut cependant lui ajouter une dimension: c'est en le pliant, en le repliant, en l'estampant, en s'étonnant que l'on satisfait son instinct du jeu, mais aussi celui du destinataire, un aspect qui ne manque pas d'intérêt. Au contraire. Si les sages japonais considèrent l'origami comme un art, ce n'est certainement pas un hasard. La fragilité de certains de ces chefs-d'œuvre filigranes est bien la preuve que toutes ces petits messages éphémères ne sont pas voués à l'éternité. □ Le destinataire se réjouit, sourit d'un air béat, soulève un instant la carte, va peut-être même jusqu'à la montrer, puis, la laisse disparaître, d'autres sensations exigeant alors toute son attention. Et pourtant: ces délicatesses passagères, chaleureuses, ne méritent-elles pas tous nos efforts, notre engagement? Pour citer Schiller encore une fois: «L'homme ne joue que lorsqu'il est homme dans tout le sens du terme et il n'est vraiment homme que lorsqu'il joue.» (Je le savais, il a bien rédigé des cartes de vœux pour Noël!) ∎

....

HERBERT LECHNER A ÉTÉ CINQ ANS RÉDACTEUR EN CHEF DU MAGAZINE SPÉCIALISÉ *GRAPHIK VISUELLES MARKETING*. IL EST AUJOURD'HUI ÉCRIVAIN ET RÉDACTEUR INDÉPENDANT À MUNICH. IL A PUBLIÉ ENTRE AUTRES UNE HISTOIRE DE LA TYPOGRAPHIE MODERNE ET UNE ÉTUDE SUR L'EMPLOI DE LA B.D. ET DE LA CARICATURE DANS LA PUBLICITÉ.

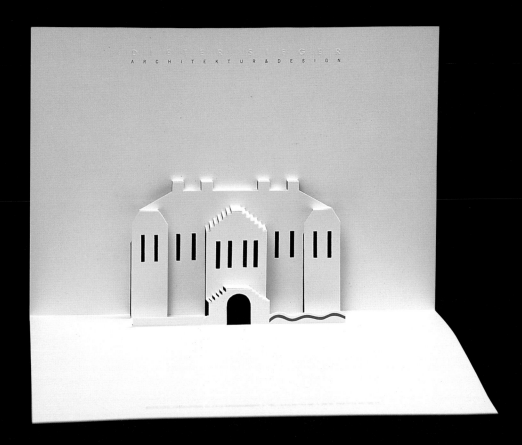

ᴇ) Aʀᴛ Dɪʀᴇᴄᴛᴏʀ: MICHAEL SIEGER Dᴇsɪɢɴᴇʀ: SIEGER DESIGN Aɢᴇɴᴄʏ: SIEGER DESIGN CONSULTING GMBH
Cʟɪᴇɴᴛ: SIEGER DESIGN Cᴏᴜɴᴛʀʏ: GERMANY □ (Oᴘᴘᴏsɪᴛᴇ ᴘᴀɢᴇ) Aʀᴛ Dɪʀᴇᴄᴛᴏʀs/Dᴇsɪɢɴᴇʀs: SUSANNA
SHANNON, JÉRÔME SAINT-LOUBERT BIÉ Aɢᴇɴᴄʏ: DESIGN DEPT. Cʟɪᴇɴᴛ: STANDARD ARCHITECTURE Cᴏᴜɴᴛʀʏ: FRANCE

Standard
architecture

Stan
dard

Fax : 43 47 23 15
Téléphone : 43 42 50 54
75011 Paris
Antoine
69, rue du Faubourg Saint

Jean et Aline Harari

arch
itec
ture

(ABOVE) ART DIRECTORS: LYNN TRICKETT, BRIAN WEBB DESIGNERS: LYNN TRICKETT, BRIAN WEBB, ANDREW THOMAS
ILLUSTRATOR/STUDIO/CLIENT: TRICKETT & WEBB LIMITED COUNTRY: GREAT BRITAIN □ (OPPOSITE) CREATIVE
DIRECTOR: KAN TAI-KEUNG ART DIRECTOR: EDDY YU CHI KONG DESIGNER: JOYCE HO NGAI SING AGENCY: KAN
TAI-KEUNG DESIGN & ASSOCIATES LTD. CLIENT: KOWLOON-CANTON RAILWAY CORPORATION COUNTRY: HONG KONG

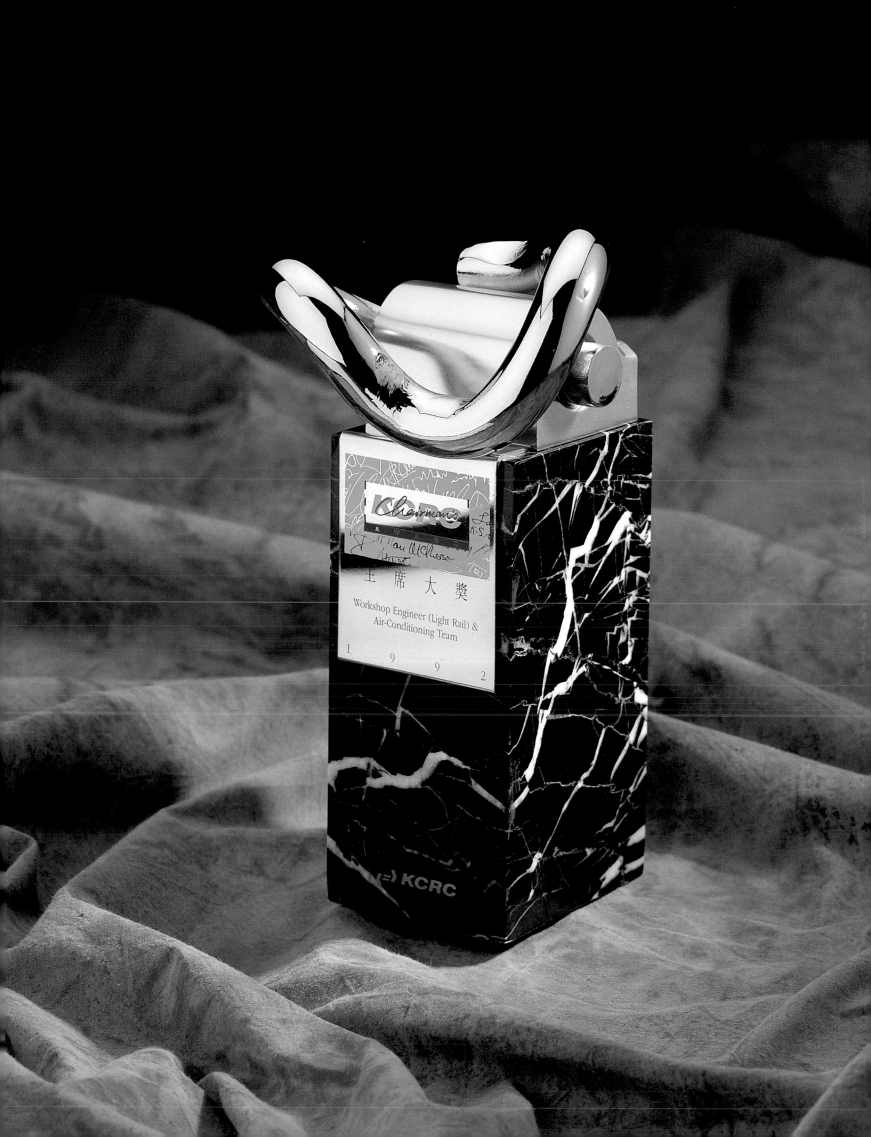

(OPPOSITE) ART DIRECTOR/DESIGNER: STEVEN JOSEPH AGENCY: SPATCHURST DESIGN ASSOCIATES CLIENT: SYDNEY ELECTRICITY COUNTRY: AUSTRALIA □ (THIS PAGE) ART DIRECTOR/DESIGNER: JOHN SAYLES COPYWRITER: WENDY LYONS AGENCY: SAYLES GRAPHIC DESIGN CLIENT: ORDER OF THE GLOBE COUNTRY: USA

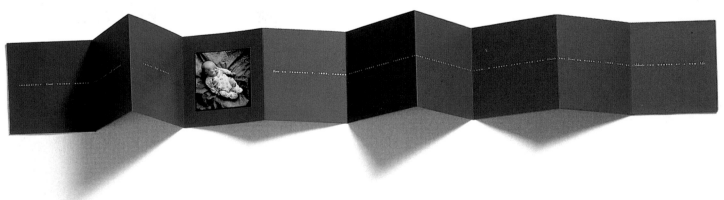

(ABOVE) ART DIRECTORS/DESIGNERS: PAT SAMATA, GREG SAMATA PHOTOGRAPHER: MARC NORBERG AGENCY: SAMATA ASSOCIATES
COUNTRY: USA □ (OPPOSITE) ART DIRECTOR/DESIGNER/PHOTOGRAPHER: JOHN CLARK AGENCY: STUDIO JOHN CLARK COUNTRY: USA

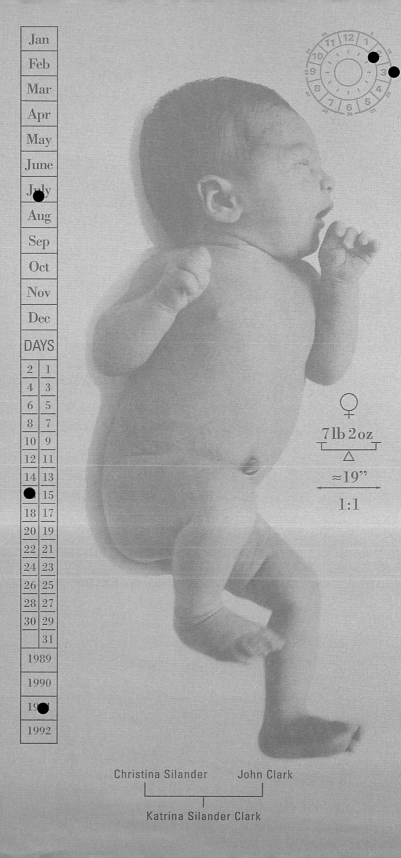

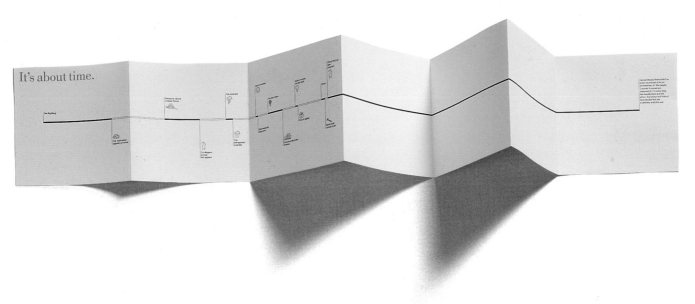

(THIS PAGE TOP) ART DIRECTORS: WILLIE BARONET, STEVE GIBBS DESIGNERS: WILLIE BARONET, META JOHNSON NEWHOUSE, KELLYE KIMBALL AGENCY: GIBBS BARONET COUNTRY: USA ☐ (THIS PAGE BOTTOM) ART DIRECTOR/DESIGNER: WOLFGANG HASLINGER COUNTRY: AUSTRIA ☐ (OPPOSITE) ART DIRECTOR/DESIGNER: ANNE MASTERS PRODUCTION COMPANIES: MCILHENNY COMPANY, DOMINO SUGAR, CAFÉ KONDITOREI SHATZ AGENCY: ANNE MASTERS DESIGN COUNTRY: USA

CATHLIN O'REILLY

PETER MÜLLER

CATHLIN O'REILLY
PETER MÜLLER

CATHLIN O'REILLY
PETER MÜLLER

CATHLIN O'REILLY
**ELENA
PETER MÜLLER**

Geboren am 24. März 1993 • Elena Livia Müller • Born on March 24, 1993

(LEFT) ART DIRECTOR/DESIGNER: IRENE MÜLLER COUNTRY: GERMANY □ (RIGHT) DESIGNER: ANDREA TILK COUNTRY:
GERMANY □ (OPPOSITE) DESIGNER: RUEDI BAUR AGENCY: INTÉGRAL RUEDI BAUR ET ASSOCIÉS COUNTRY: FRANCE

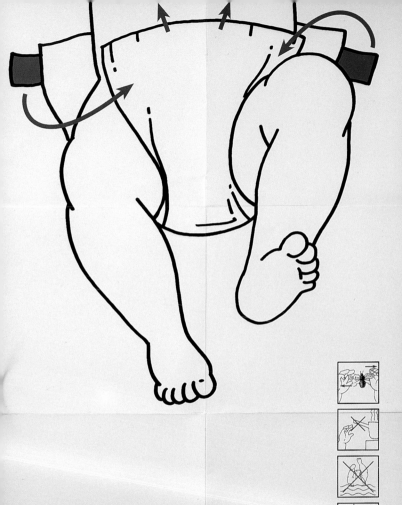

Danièle et Denis
sont heureux de vous
apprendre la naissance de
Valentin, Sylvie,
Gaël Alba-Arnau,
né le 14 juin 1993.

16 rue de l'Helvétie
74100 Ambilly
tel 50 38 39 98

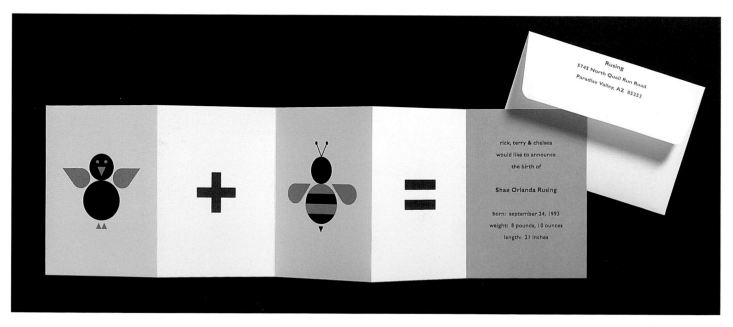

(TOP) ART DIRECTOR/DESIGNER/PHOTOGRAPHER: ALAN BROOKS COPYWRITERS: HEATHER BROOKS, ALAN BROOKS AGENCY: BROOKS CHAMPION INC. COUNTRY: USA □ (BOTTOM) ART DIRECTORS/DESIGNERS: STEVE DITKO, MIKE CAMPBELL ILLUSTRATOR: MARISSA BENINCASA AGENCY: CAMPBELL FISHER DITKO DESIGN COUNTRY: USA □ (OPPOSITE TOP) ART DIRECTOR/DESIGNER/PHOTOGRAPHER: PETER R. BITTER AGENCY: BITTER AGENTUR FÜR WERBUNG UND KOMMUNI-KATION COUNTRY: GERMANY □ (BOTTOM) ART DIRECTOR/DESIGNER/PHOTOGRAPHER: IVO VON RENNER COUNTRY: GERMANY

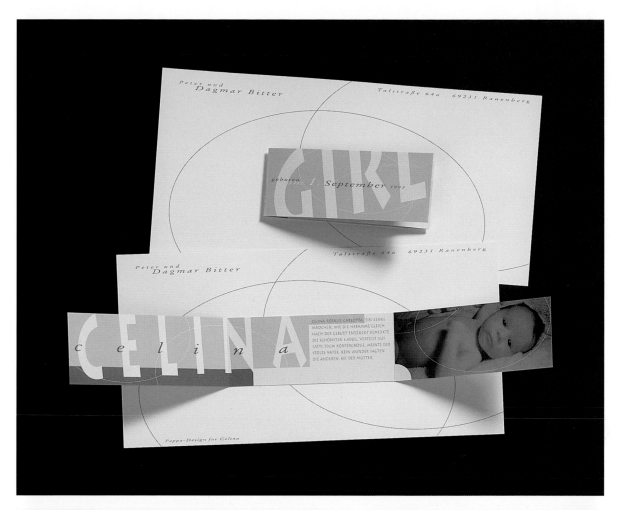

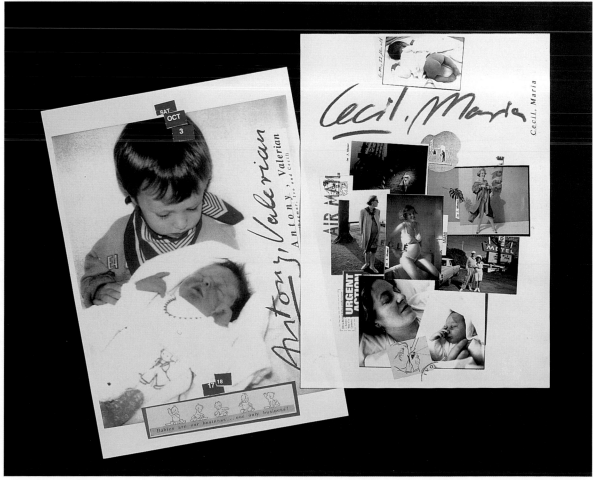

In Denmark and Sweden there is a custom of baking a Yule boar at Christmas. This custom began with the pagan belief that a benificent grain spirit existed within their crops. To embody this spirit throughout the winter, ancient Scandinavians used the flour from the last sheaf harvested to bake

a boar-shaped loaf — the boar symbolized their god of re... ...g and sowing pieces of the Yule boar at spring planting, the grain spirit was returned to the crops to ensure a bountiful harvest. T... ...ay b... ...n the original boaring winter. *Have a wonderful 1994.* M. Skjei Design Co.

X is for Xmas
because X is part
of the ancient
greek Chrismon,
Christ's monogram.

X referes also
to the Roman
numeral ten = X
This X is for break
into the final
decennium of the
20th century.

Merry Xmas
and a very Happy
New Year

Bruno & Ruth Wiese

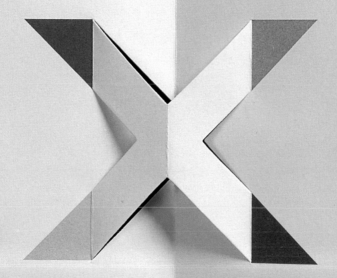

Bruno & Ruth Wiese

Frohe Weihnachten
und ein sehr
glückliches 1990

X als römische Zehn
steht hier auch
für den Anbruch
des letzten
Dezenniums dieses
Jahrhunderts.

X ist Teil des
altgriechischen
Chrismons, des
Christusmonogramms.
So auch in 'Xmas'
anstelle von Christmas.

(THIS SPREAD) ART DIRECTOR: JEFF MILSTEIN DESIGNER: JEFF MILSTEIN ILLUSTRATOR: JEFF MILSTEIN AGENCY: JEFF MILSTEIN STUDIO CLIENT: MUSEUM OF MODERN ART COUNTRY: USA

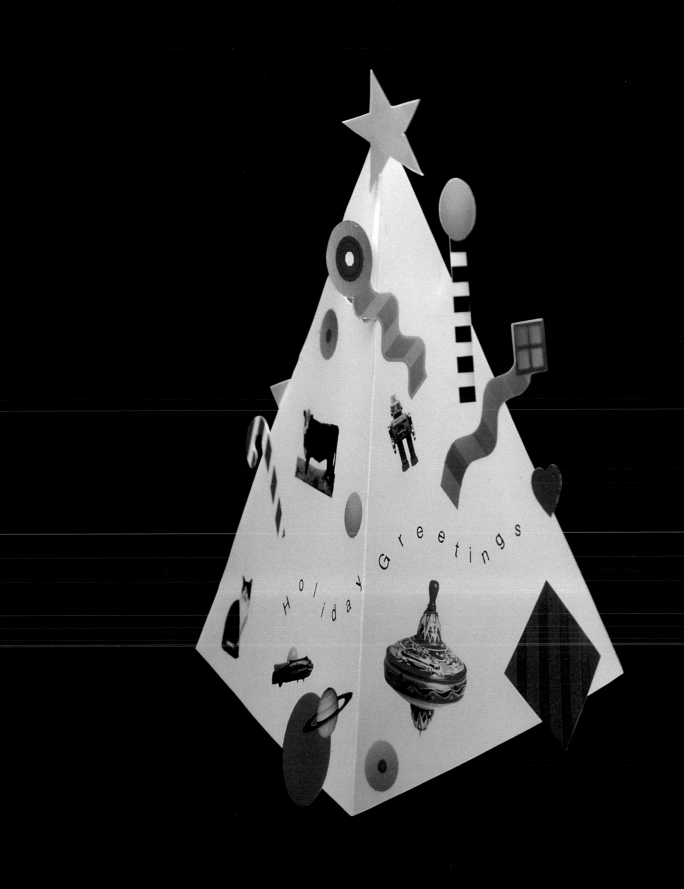

Holiday Greetings

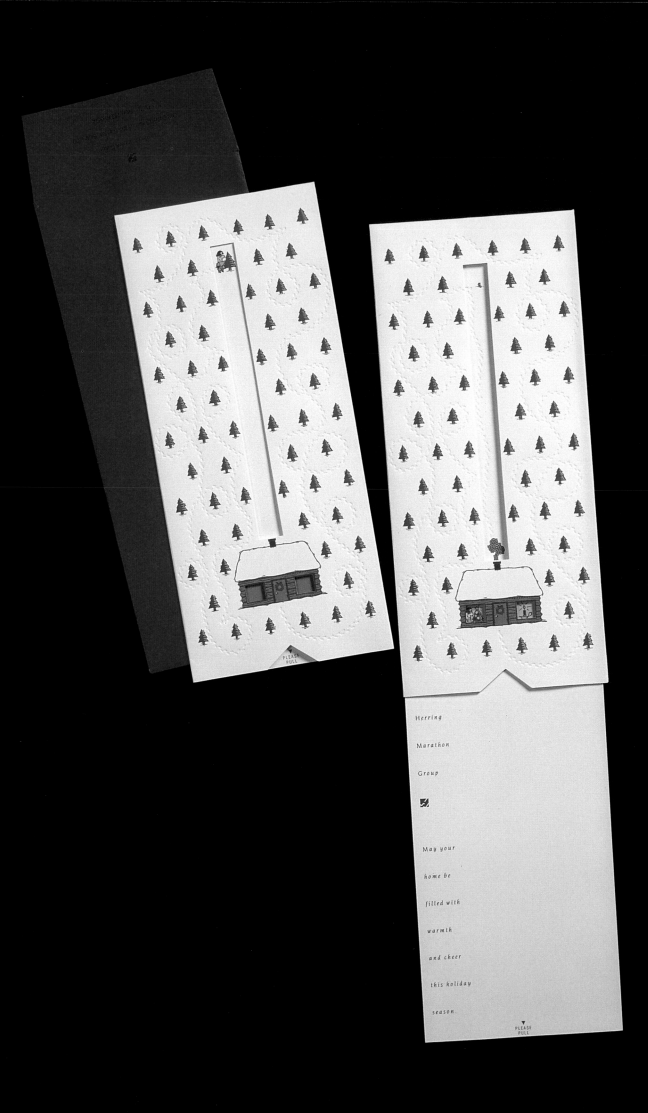

Herring

Marathon

Group

May your

home be

filled with

warmth

and cheer

this holiday

season.

PLEASE
PULL

Shiny runners whisper through the snow,

A Christmas sled, remembered, long ago,

All varnished pride and swift, it brought

The wind's cold kiss, and little sister

Waiting for her ride. The tug and struggle

Up the slope, mittens frozen to the rope.

A rush and flop—and we had wings again! Until

At last, the sun has disappeared behind the hill. Then

Home we trudged. Contented. Frozen in the fading light,

Our runnered glory set upright, outside the door,

To soar another day....

This season, which makes memory bright,

We wish you all a child's delight.

A hill that's gentle, run that's clear,

The joy of childhood through the year....   Cook and Shanosky Associates Inc.

(OPPOSITE) ART DIRECTOR/DESIGNER/COPYWRITER: BOB DENNARD ILLUSTRATOR: BRAD WINES AGENCY: DENNARD CREATIVE, INC. CLIENT: HERRING MARATHON GROUP COUNTRY: USA ☐ (THIS PAGE) ART DIRECTOR/DESIGNER/PHOTOGRAPHER: ROGER COOK COPYWRITER: DAVID L. EYNON AGENCY/CLIENT: COOK AND SHANOSKY ASSOCIATES, INC. COUNTRY: USA

**PACKING IS ONLY
PROTECTIVE FOR
THE ORIGINAL.**

DIE KLEINE
WEIHNACHTSFEIER.

BITTE LÖSEN.

BITTE ZÜNDEN.

WIR WÜNSCHEN IHNEN
EIN FROHES FEST UND
EIN GUTES NEUES JAHR.

Perfect.

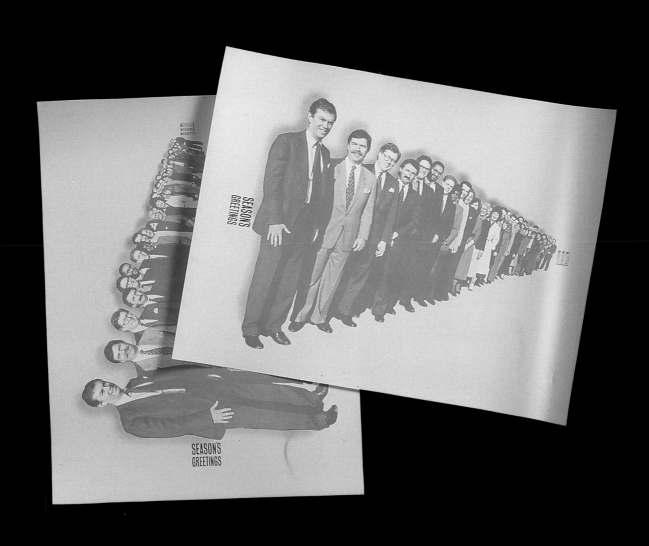

(Above) Art Director: SEYMOUR CHWAST Designer: GREG SIMPSON Photographer: SCOTT STERNBACH Agency: THE
PUSHPIN GROUP Client: BUTLER ROGERS BASKETT Country: USA □ (Opposite) Art Director/Illustrator: BRUNO
HAAG Designer: THOMAS HENSCHKE Agency/Client: BRUNO HAAG KONZEPTION & ART DIRECTION Country: GERMANY

Tolerance

Understanding

Peace

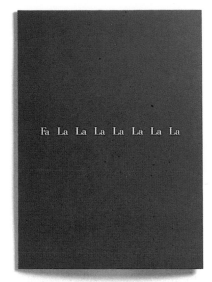
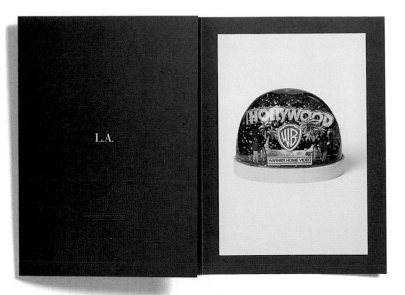

(OPPOSITE) ART DIRECTOR/DESIGNER/CLIENT: DEWITT KENDALL AGENCY: DEWITT KENDALL-CHICAGO COUNTRY: USA □ (THIS PAGE TOP) ART DIRECTOR: MICHAEL BROCK DESIGNER: MICHAEL BROCK PHOTOGRAPHER: TOM KELLER AGENCY: MICHAEL BROCK DESIGN CLIENT: WARNER HOME VIDEO COUNTRY: USA □ (BOTTOM) ART DIRECTOR: ERIC RICKA-BAUGH DESIGNER: MICHAEL SMITH ILLUSTRATOR: MICHAEL SMITH AGENCY/CLIENT: RICKABAUGH GRAPHICS COUNTRY: USA

DIDIER LECOINTRE
DOMINIQUE DROUET
VOUS SOUHAITENT
UNE BONNE ANNÉE

(THIS PAGE) ART DIRECTOR: PHILIPPE GHIELMETTI DESIGNER: PHILIPPE GHIELMETTI AGENCY: SKETCH STUDIO CLIENTS: DIDIER LECOINTRE, DENIS OZANNE COUNTRY: FRANCE □ (OPPOSITE PAGE) ART DIRECTOR: DAVID LERCH DESIGNER/ILLUSTRATOR: DAVID LERCH COPYWRITER: LISA LERCH AGENCY/CLIENT: PENNEBAKER DESIGN COUNTRY: USA

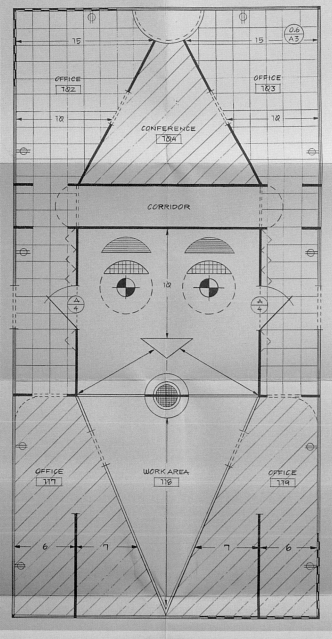

OFFICE 102

OFFICE 103

CONFERENCE 104

CORRIDOR

OFFICE 117

WORK AREA 118

OFFICE 119

PENNEBAKER **D**ESIGN

WISHES **Y**OU **A**ND **Y**OURS

V **M**ERRY **C**HRISTMAS

FROM **O**UR **N**EW **O**FFICES

AT 4801 **W**OODWAY, **S**UITE 280E

may the peace of this joyous season

carry you through the new year

michael brock design

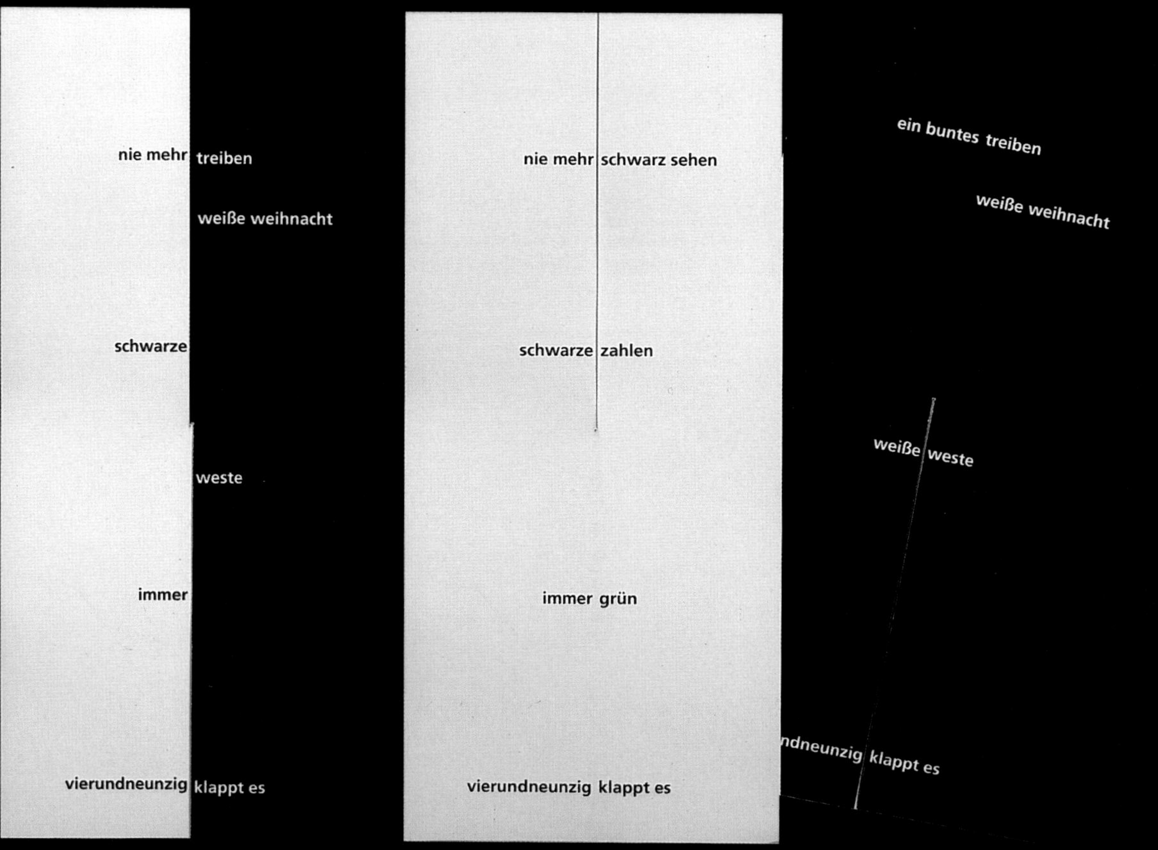

nie mehr treiben

weiße weihnacht

schwarze

weste

immer

vierundneunzig klappt es

nie mehr schwarz sehen

schwarze zahlen

immer grün

vierundneunzig klappt es

ein buntes treiben

weiße weihnacht

weiße weste

ndneunzig klappt es

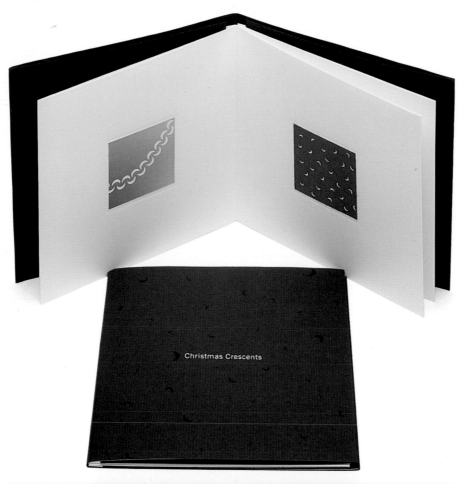

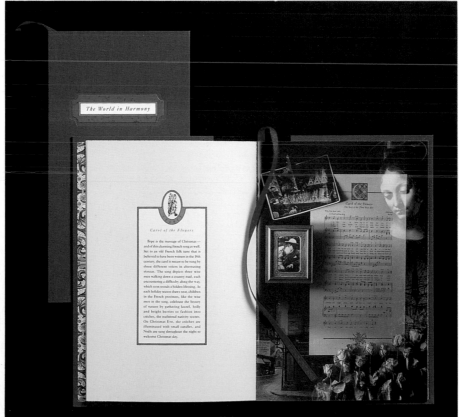

(THIS PAGE TOP) ART DIRECTOR/DESIGNER: LYNDA BROCKBANK AGENCY/CLIENT: CRESCENT LODGE DESIGN COUNTRY: GREAT
BRITAIN ☐ (THIS PAGE BOTTOM) ART DIRECTOR: DAVID CARTER DESIGNER: RANDALL HILL PHOTOGRAPHER: KLEIN
+ WILSON COPYWRITER: MARSHA COBURN AGENCY/CLIENT: DAVID CARTER GRAPHIC DESIGN ASSOCIATES COUNTRY: USA

(ABOVE) ART DIRECTOR/DESIGNER: WOLFGANG HASLINGER COUNTRY: AUSTRIA □ (OPPOSITE) ART DIRECTORS: KARI PALMQVIST,
JEANETTE PALMQVIST DESIGNER/ILLUSTRATOR: KARI PALMQVIST AGENCY/CLIENT: BUBBLAN STUDIO COUNTRY: SWEDEN

50

SKÖN SOMMAR

STUDIO BUBBLAN

GOD JUL

GOTT NYTT ÅR

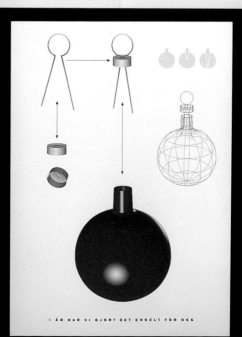

I ÅR HAR VI GJORT DET ENKELT FÖR OSS

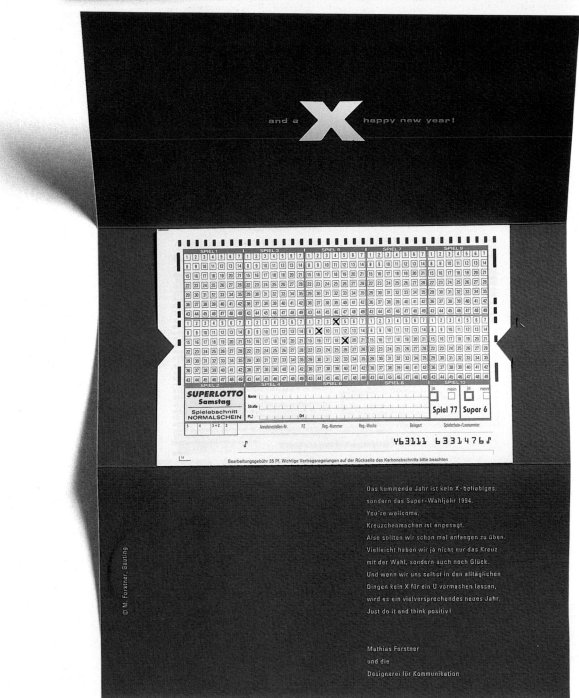

Das kommende Jahr ist kein X-beliebiges,

sondern das Super-Wahljahr 1994.

You're wellcome.

Kreuzchenmachen ist angesagt.

Also sollten wir schon mal anfangen zu üben.

Vielleicht haben wir ja nicht nur das Kreuz

mit der Wahl, sondern auch noch Glück.

Und wenn wir uns selbst in den alltäglichen

Dingen kein X für ein U vormachen lassen,

wird es ein vielversprechendes neues Jahr.

Just do it and think positiv!

Mathias Forstner

und die

Designerei für Kommunikation

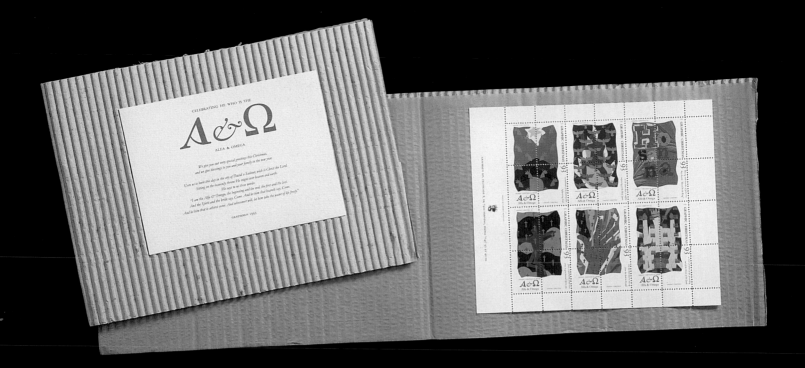

(Opposite) Art Director/Designer: MATHIAS FORSTNER Agency/Client: DESIGNEREI F. KOMMUNIKATION Country: GERMANY □ (This page top) Art Director/Designer/Illustrator: CARSTEN SKOVLUND Agency/Client: GRAFIKKEN Country: DENMARK □ (This page bottom left) Art Director: GARRY EMERY Designer/Agency/Client: EMERY VINCENT ASSOCIATES Country: AUSTRALIA □ (This page bottom right) Art Director/Designer/Photographer/Illustrator: KENNETH KARLSSON Agency/Client: ATELJÉ ELEFANTEN & FARET AB Country: SWEDEN

(OPPOSITE) ART DIRECTOR: JENNIFER MORLA DESIGNERS: JENNIFER MORLA, CRAIG BAILEY AGENCY/CLIENT: MORLA DESIGN COUNTRY:

USA □ (ABOVE) ART DIRECTOR/DESIGNER: R.O. BLECHMAN AGENCY: R.O. BLECHMAN, INC. CLIENT: THE INK TANK COUNTRY: USA

(THIS PAGE TOP) ART DIRECTOR/DESIGNER: MICHAEL BROCK PHOTOGRAPHER: TOM KELLER AGENCY/CLIENT: MICHAEL BROCK
DESIGN COUNTRY: USA □ (THIS PAGE BOTTOM) ART DIRECTOR: PIER PAOLO PITALLO ILLUSTRATOR: PAOLO D'ALTAN
AGENCY: CENTO PER CENTO COUNTRY: ITALY □ (OPPOSITE PAGE) ART DIRECTORS: BOB HAMBLY, BARBARA
WOOLLEY DESIGNERS: BOB HAMBLY, BARBARA WOOLLEY AGENCY/CLIENT: HAMBLY & WOOLLEY INC. COUNTRY: CANADA

MARIA CRISTINA ROMAGNOLI · GRAFICA · VIA MASSACIUCCOLI 12 00199 ROMA TEL 06/ 86.21.82.60

(OPPOSITE PAGE) ART DIRECTOR: ROLAND SCHNEIDER DESIGNER: MICHAELA BAUER AGENCY: BAUERS BÜRO CLIENT: FASHION
STAGE COUNTRY: GERMANY □ (ABOVE) ART DIRECTOR/DESIGNER/CLIENT: MARIA CRISTINA ROMAGNOLI COUNTRY: ITALY

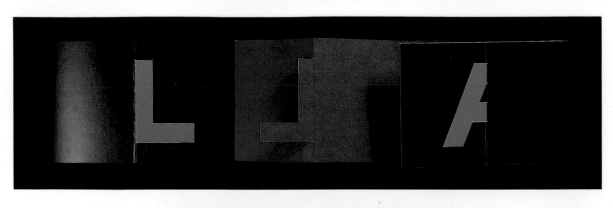

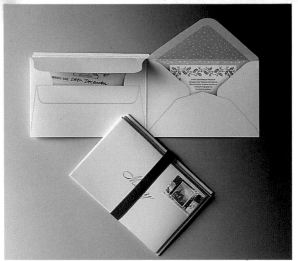

(THIS PAGE TOP) ART DIRECTOR: JULIA CHONG TAM DESIGNER: JULIA CHONG TAM ILLUSTRATOR: JULIA CHONG TAM AGENCY/CLIENT: JULIA TAM DESIGN COUNTRY: USA □ (THIS PAGE BOTTOM) ART DIRECTORS: LYNN TRICKETT, BRIAN WEBB DESIGNERS: LYNN TRICKETT, BRIAN WEBB, ANDREW THOMAS ILLUSTRATORS/STUDIO/CLIENT: TRICKETT & WEBB LIMITED COUNTRY: GREAT BRITAIN □ (OPPOSITE PAGE) ART DIRECTOR: BYRON JACOBS DESIGNERS: BYRON JACOBS, MICHELLE SHEK ILLUSTRATOR: PPA DESIGN LIMITED AGENCY/CLIENT: PPA DESIGN LIMITED COUNTRY: HONG KONG

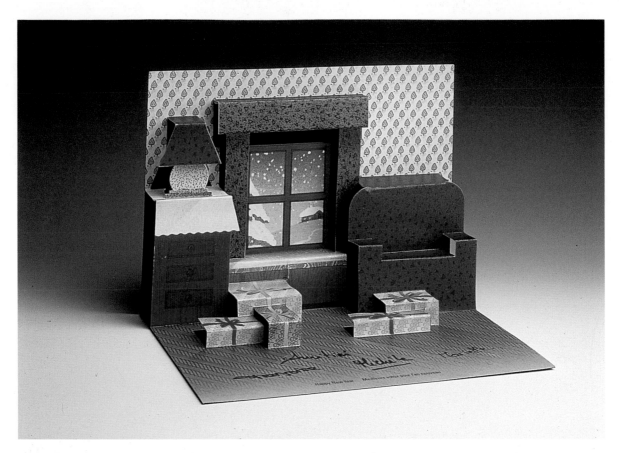

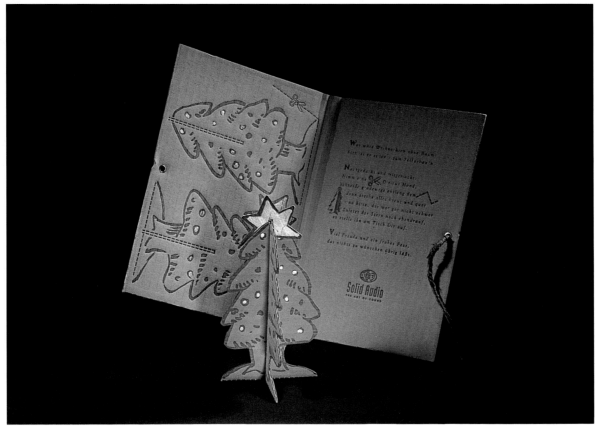

(THIS PAGE TOP) ART DIRECTOR/DESIGNER: EDUARD CEHOVIN PHOTOGRAPHER: BORIS GABERSCEK AGENCY: M DESIGN CLIENT: EBEL MONTRES SA COUNTRY: SWITZERLAND □ (THIS PAGE BOTTOM) ART DIRECTOR/DESIGNER/ILLUSTRATOR: WOLFGANG HASLINGER CLIENT: SOLID AUDIO COUNTRY: AUSTRIA □ (OPPOSITE PAGE) ART DIRECTORS/DESIGNERS: JEFF LARSON, SCOTT JOHNSON COPYWRITER: JEFF LARSON AGENCY/CLIENT: LARSON DESIGN ASSOCIATES COUNTRY: USA

(ᴬᴳᴱ ᴛᴼᴾ) Aʀᴛ Dɪʀᴇᴄᴛᴏʀ: JOSE SERRANO Dᴇsɪɢɴᴇʀ: JOSE SERRANO Iʟʟᴜsᴛʀᴀᴛᴏʀ: MIRES DESIGN STAFF Aɢᴇɴᴄʏ:
MIRES DESIGN Cʟɪᴇɴᴛ: MIRES DESIGN Cᴏᴜɴᴛʀʏ: USA ◻ (Tʜɪs ᴘᴀɢᴇ ᴄᴇɴᴛᴇʀ ᴀɴᴅ ʙᴏᴛᴛᴏᴍ) Aʀᴛ Dɪʀᴇᴄᴛᴏʀ/Dᴇsɪɢɴᴇʀ:
JULIA CHONG TAM Iʟʟᴜsᴛʀᴀᴛᴏʀ: JULIA CHONG TAM Aɢᴇɴᴄʏ/Cʟɪᴇɴᴛ: JULIA TAM DESIGN Cᴏᴜɴᴛʀʏ: USA ◻
(Oᴘᴘᴏsɪᴛᴇ ᴛᴏᴘ ʟᴇғᴛ) Aʀᴛ Dɪʀᴇᴄᴛᴏʀs: LO BREIER, ANDREAS MIEDANER Dᴇsɪɢɴᴇʀ: CARL VAN OMMEN Aɢᴇɴᴄʏ/Cʟɪᴇɴᴛ: BÜ◻

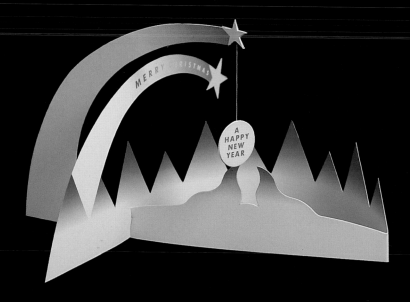

COUNTRY: GERMANY □ (THIS PAGE TOP RIGHT) ART DIRECTOR: JOHN PARHAM DESIGNER/ILLUSTRATOR: MARUCHI SANTANA AGENCY/CLIENT: PARHAM SANTANA DESIGN COUNTRY: USA □ (THIS PAGE CENTER) ART DIRECTOR: BARBARA BORGSTÄDT DESIGNER/AGENCY: BARBARA BORGSTÄDT ILLUSTRATOR: UWE OCHSLER COUNTRY: GERMANY □ (THIS PAGE BOTTOM) ART DIRECTOR/DESIGNER: KEISUKE UNOSAWA AGENCY/CLIENT: KEISUKE UNOSAWA DESIGN COUNTRY: JAPAN

GIFTWRAP

GIFTWRAP

PRIMO ANGELI

PRIMO ANGELI

NO. OF 700 SETS

NO. OF 700 SETS

(OPPOSITE PAGE) ART DIRECTOR/DESIGNER: PRIMO ANGELI CLIENT: PRIMO ANGELI INC. COUNTRY: USA □ (THIS PAGE) ART
DIRECTORS: MIKE HICKS, TOM POTH DESIGNERS: MIKE HICKS, MATT HECK AGENCY/CLIENT: HIXO, INC. COUNTRY: USA

(THIS PAGE TOP) ART DIRECTORS/DESIGNERS/CLIENTS: MARTINA EISELEIN, HEIKE SCHIRMER PHOTOGRAPHER: DIETMAR HORNUNG COUNTRY: GERMANY □ (THIS PAGE BOTTOM) ART DIRECTOR/DESIGNER: KEISUKE UNOSAWA AGENCY/CLIENT: KEISUKE UNOSAWA DESIGN COUNTRY: JAPAN □ (OPPOSITE) ART DIRECTOR/DESIGNER/CLIENT: DAVID TARTAKOVER AGENCY: TARTAKOVER DESIGN COUNTRY: ISRAEL □ (FOLLOWING SPREAD LEFT) DESIGNERS: TODD WATERBURY, SHARON WERNER CONSTRUCTION DESIGNER: BERNIE LECLERC ILLUSTRATORS: LYNN SCHULTE, TODD WATERBURY, SHARON WERNER AGENCY/CLIENT: DUFFY, INC. COUNTRY: USA □ (FOLLOWING SPREAD RIGHT) ART DIRECTOR: GARRY EMERY DESIGNER/AGENCY: EMERY VINCENT ASSOCIATES CLIENT: CARMEN FURNITURE (SALES) PTY LTD. COUNTRY: AUSTRALIA

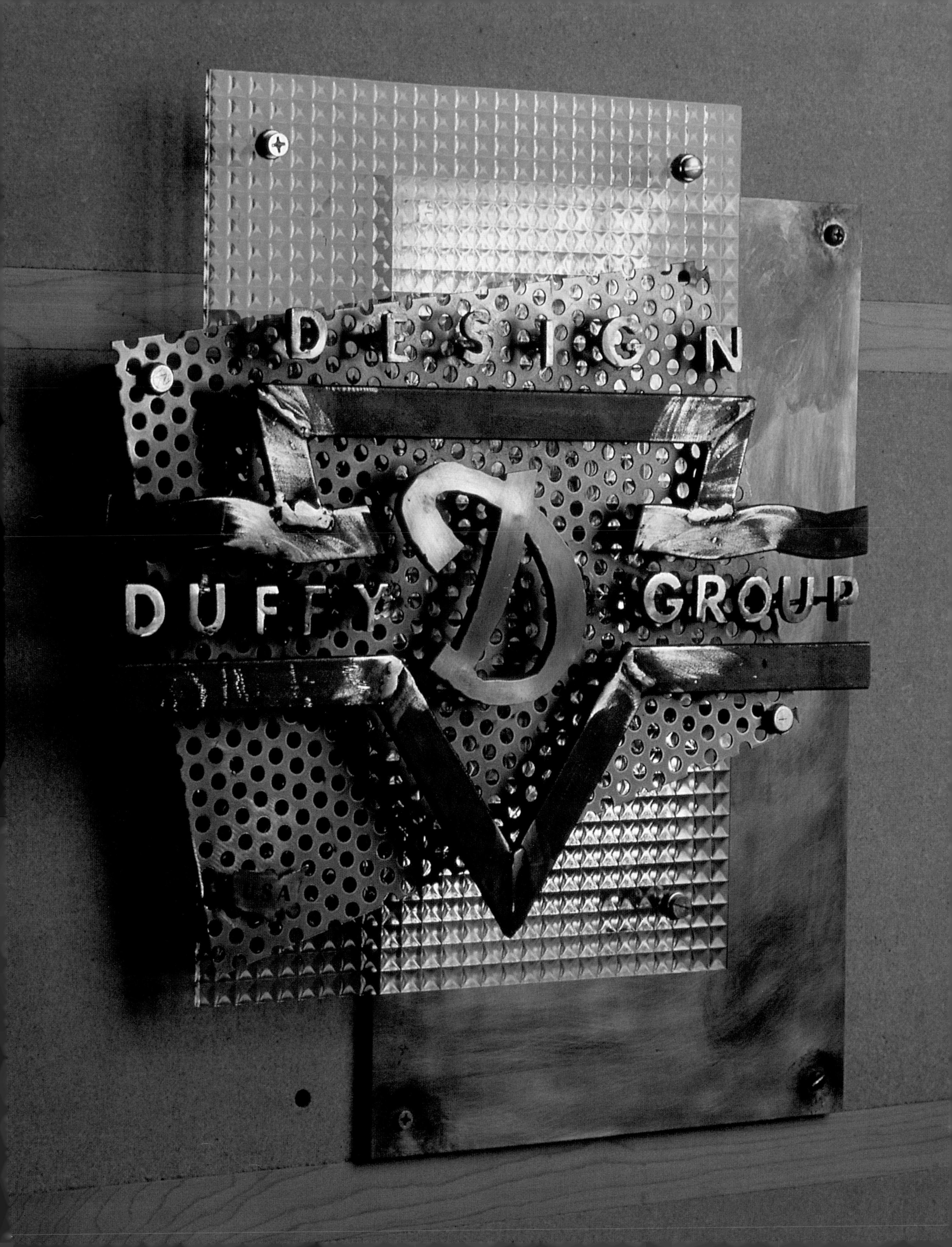
DESIGN
DUFFY
GROUP

(OPPOSITE) ART DIRECTOR: CHARLES S. ANDERSON DESIGNERS: CHARLES S. ANDERSON, TODD HAUSWIRTH PHOTOGRAPHER: DARRELL EAGER ILLUSTRATOR: CSA ARCHIVE AGENCY/CLIENT: CHARLES S. ANDERSON DESIGN CO. COUNTRY: USA □ (THIS PAGE TOP) ART DIRECTOR/DESIGNER: BARRIE TUCKER AGENCY/CLIENT: TUCKER DESIGN COUNTRY: AUSTRALIA □ (BOTTOM) ART DIRECTOR/DESIGNER: CLIVE H. GAY PHOTOGRAPHER: ROLAND MEISSNER AGENCY/CLIENT: TRADEMARK DESIGN COUNTRY: SOUTH AFRICA

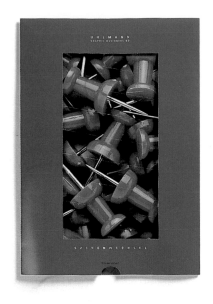
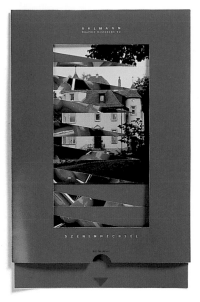
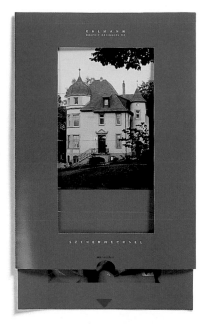

(TOP) ART DIRECTOR/DESIGNER: MONIKA UHLMANN PHOTOGRAPHERS: FOTOSTUDIO KONRAD HOFFMANN, COSMO-TONE (BACKGROUND) CLIENT: UHLMANN GRAPHICDESIGNERS COUNTRY: GERMANY ☐ (BOTTOM) ART DIRECTOR/ DESIGNER: CHARLES HIVELY AGENCY/CLIENT: THE HIVELY AGENCY, INC. COUNTRY: USA ☐ (OPPOSITE) ART DIRECTOR/DESIGNER: SHARON WERNER AGENCY: DUFFY, INC. CLIENT: FOX RIVER PAPER COMPANY COUNTRY: USA

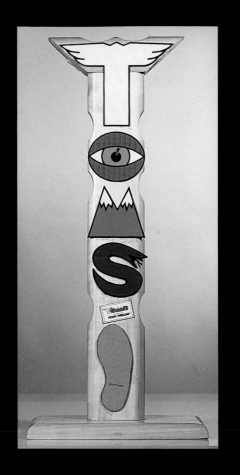

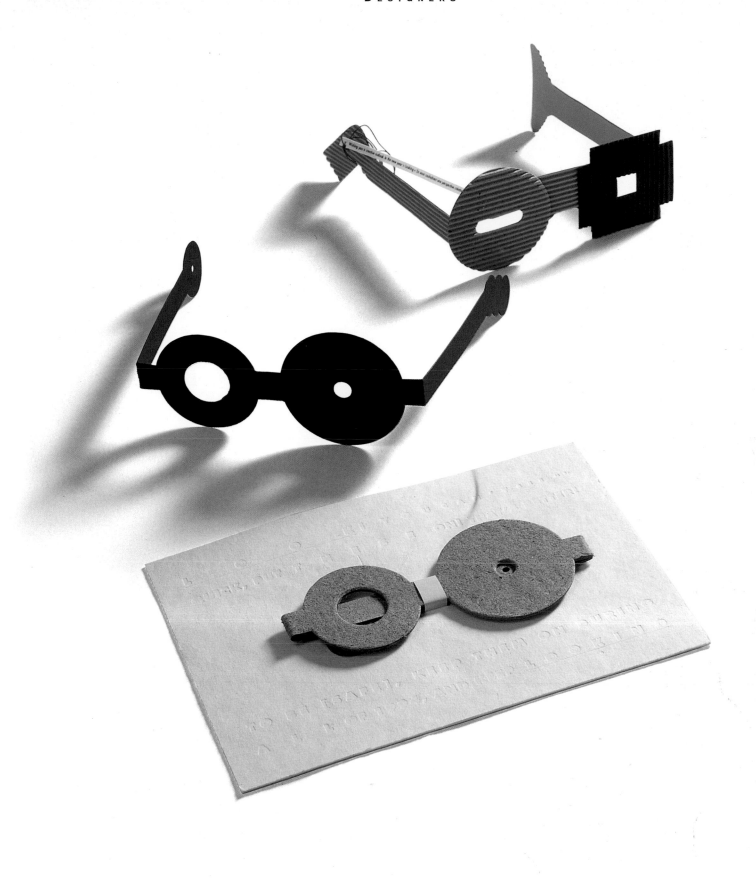

(Opposite top) Art Directors: CORNELIA STOFFREGEN, JOSEF SCHEWE Photographer: FRIEDRUN REINHOLD Agency: DIE WERBEAGENTUR FFF Client: TERRANO SCHUH GMBH Country: GERMANY □ (Bottom) Art Director: KEISUKE UNOSAWA Designer: KEISUKE UNOSAWA Agency: KEISUKE UNOSAWA DESIGN Client: KEISUKE UNOSAWA DESIGN Country: JAPAN □ (Above) Art Director: JOHN CLARK Designer: JOHN CLARK Agency/Client: LOOKING Country: USA

(THIS PAGE) **1** ART DIRECTOR/DESIGNER: BRUCE EDWARDS ILLUSTRATOR: MICHAEL SCHWAB AGENCY: RAPP COLLINS COMMUNI-
CATIONS CLIENT: KATHRYN BEICH (NESTLE-BEICH'S FUNDRAISING) COUNTRY: USA □ (OPPOSITE, FROM TOP LEFT TO
BOTTOM RIGHT) **2, 5** ART DIRECTOR: CHARLES S. ANDERSON DESIGNERS: CHARLES S. ANDERSON, DANIEL OLSON
PHOTOGRAPHER: PAUL IRMITER AGENCY/CLIENT: CHARLES S. ANDERSON DESIGN CO. COUNTRY: USA □ **3** ART
DIRECTOR/DESIGNER: JOSE SERRANO PHOTOGRAPHER: CARL VANDERSCHUIT ILLUSTRATOR: TRACY SABIN AGENCY:
MIRES DESIGN, INC. CLIENT: BORDEAUX PRINTERS COUNTRY: USA □ **4** ART DIRECTOR/DESIGNER: BARRY A.
MERTEN PHOTOGRAPHER: DOUG STEWART AGENCY: MERTEN DESIGN GROUP CLIENT: MERTEN DESIGN GROUP COUNTRY: USA

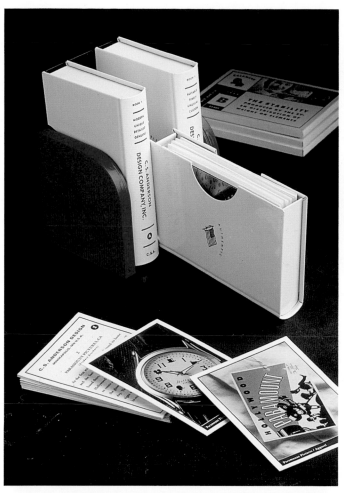

(THIS PAGE) ART DIRECTOR: CAROL HOOVER DESIGNERS: CAROL HOOVER, MICHAEL HINSHAW AGENCY/CLIENT: TRIAD, INC.
COUNTRY: USA □ (OPPOSITE PAGE) ART DIRECTOR: THOMAS OTTE DESIGNER: INES KASPER COPYWRITER: CLAUDIA
LANDWEHR AGENCY: STIEHL/OTTE WERBEAGENTUR GMBH CLIENT: STIEHL/OTTE WERBEAGENTUR GMBH COUNTRY: GERMANY

LIEBER HERR SCHNEIDEWIND!

WENN SIE EINMAL
MIT IHRER AGENTUR
LIEGENBLEIBEN,
IST ES GUT, EINE
RESERVE ZU HABEN,
DIE SIE WIEDER
VORANBRINGT.

VIELLEICHT SOGAR BIS OSNABRÜCK.
STIEHL / OTTE

(THIS PAGE) ART DIRECTORS: ROBYNNE RAYE, VITTORIO COSTARELLA DESIGNERS: ROBYNNE RAYE, VITTORIO COSTARELLA, MICHAEL STRASSBURGER AGENCY/CLIENT: MODERN DOG COUNTRY: USA □ (OPPOSITE, FROM TOP LEFT TO BOTTOM RIGHT) **1** ART DIRECTOR/DESIGNER: THOMAS G. FOWLER AGENCY: TOM FOWLER, INC. CLIENT: GRAPHICS 3 COUNTRY: USA □ **2** ART DIRECTOR/DESIGNER: KAREN MURRAY AGENCY/CLIENT: DESIGNWORKS COUNTRY: NEW ZEALAND □ **3** ART DIRECTOR/DESIGNER: WOLFGANG HASLINGER COUNTRY: AUSTRIA □ **4** ART DIRECTOR: HUGO PUTTAERT DESIGNERS: HUGO PUTTAERT, JOHAN JACOBS, POL QUADENS AGENCY/CLIENT: VISION & FACTORY COUNTRY: BELGIUM □ **5** DESIGNERS: FRANCISCO RIOS, JIM MOUSNER AGENCY/CLIENT: TRIBE! DESIGN COUNTRY: USA □ **6** ART DIRECTION: (Z)OO PRODUKTIES, ANITA STEKETEE DESIGNERS/ILLUSTRATORS: VARIOUS AGENCY/CLIENT: (Z)OO PRODUKTIES, ERIC VAN CASTEREN, ROBERT VAN RIXTEL COUNTRY: NETHERLANDS □ **7** ART DIRECTOR/ DESIGNER: GRANT JORGENSEN COPYWRITER: ROGER LIMINTON AGENCY: GRANT JORGENSEN DESIGN CLIENT: LIMINTON CORCORAN DESIGN COUNTRY: AUSTRALIA □ **8** ART DIRECTOR/DESIGNER: WOLFGANG HASLINGER COUNTRY: AUSTRIA □ (FOLLOWING SPREAD LEFT) ART DIRECTORS: STEVE WEDEEN, RICK VAUGHN, DANIEL MICHAEL FLYNN DESIGNER: DANIEL MICHAEL FLYNN ILLUSTRATOR: BILL GERHOLD AGENCY/CLIENT: VAUGHN WEDEEN CREATIVE COUNTRY: USA □ (FOLLOWING SPREAD RIGHT) ART DIRECTOR: BARRIE TUCKER DESIGNERS: BARRIE TUCKER, HANS KOHLA AGENCY: TUCKER DESIGN CLIENT: WOODS BAGOT COUNTRY: AUSTRALIA

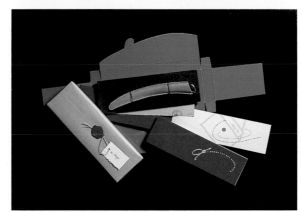

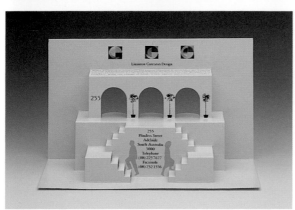

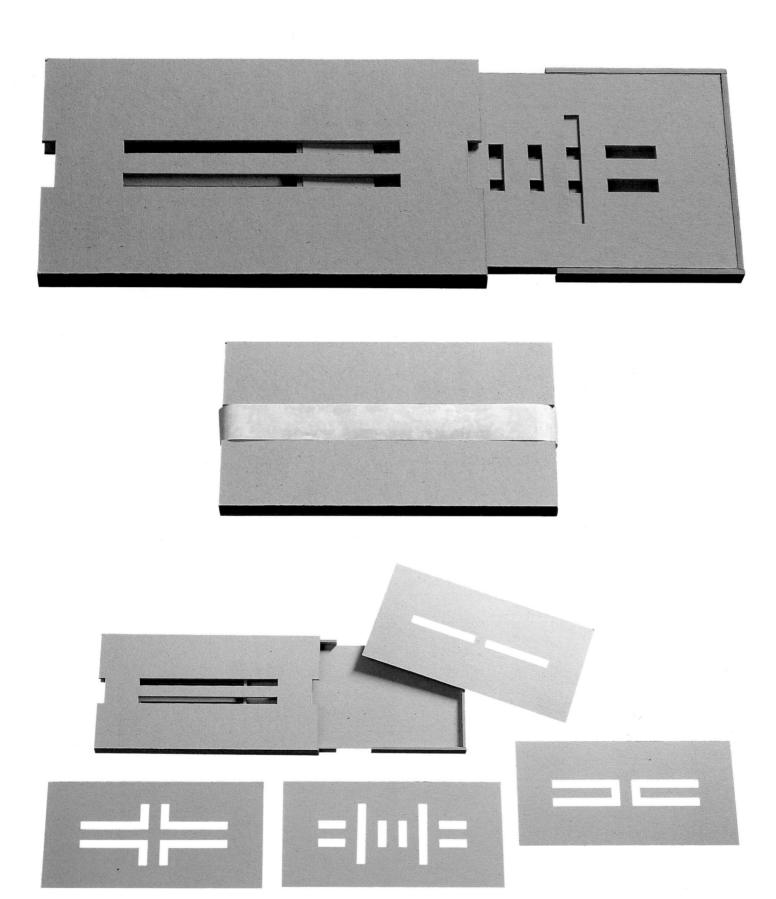

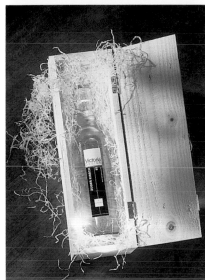

(OPPOSITE) ART DIRECTOR/DESIGNER/AGENCY/CLIENT: RALF STUTZ COUNTRY: GERMANY □ (ABOVE, TOP LEFT) ART DIRECTOR: RICK VAUGHN DESIGNER/ILLUSTRATOR: DANIEL MICHAEL FLYNN AGENCY/CLIENT: VAUGHN WEDEEN CREATIVE COUNTRY: USA □ (BOTTOM LEFT) ART DIRECTOR: URS J. KNOBEL DESIGNER: KARIN BIRCHLER AGENCY: URS J. KNOBEL WERBUNG CLIENT: VICTORIA WERKE AG, MÖBELFABRIK COUNTRY: SWITZERLAND □ (CENTER) ART DIRECTOR/ DESIGNER: BARRIE TUCKER AGENCY: TUCKER DESIGN CLIENT: AVON GRAPHICS COUNTRY: AUSTRALIA □ (TOP RIGHT) ART DIRECTOR/DESIGNER: CHUCK ANDERSON ILLUSTRATOR: LYNN SCHULTE AGENCY/CLIENT: DUFFY, INC. COUNTRY: USA □ (BOTTOM RIGHT) ART DIRECTOR/DESIGNER: KURT MEINECKE AGENCY/CLIENT: GROUP/CHICAGO, INC. COUNTRY: USA

(THIS PAGE LEFT) ART DIRECTOR: CHARLES S. ANDERSON DESIGNERS: CHARLES S. ANDERSON, TODD HAUSWIRTH PHOTOGRAPHER: DARRELL EAGER AGENCY: CHARLES S. ANDERSON DESIGN CO. CLIENT: PRINT CRAFT, INC. COUNTRY: USA □ (THIS PAGE RIGHT) ART DIRECTOR: CHARLES S. ANDERSON DESIGNERS: CHARLES S. ANDERSON, TODD HAUSWIRTH PHOTOGRAPHER: PAUL IRMITER ILLUSTRATOR: CSA ARCHIVE AGENCY: CHARLES S. ANDERSON DESIGN CO. CLIENT: FRENCH PAPER CO. COUNTRY: USA □ (OPPOSITE) ART DIRECTOR/DESIGNER: CARTER WEITZ WRITER: MITCH KOCH AGENCY: BAILEY LAUERMAN & ASSOCIATES CLIENT: WESTERN PAPER COMPANY COUNTRY: USA

UP ON THE ROOFTOP, SIP... SIP... SIP

PARTY'S UNFOLDING WITH OLE ST. NICK.

THURSDAY
DECEMBER 17, 1987
5:30 P.M. TO 8:30 P.M.
2424 SOUTH DIXIE HIGHWAY
MIAMI, FLORIDA

DIXON & FRIEDMAN
PANORAMA DESIGN
MAYTE REID
DANIEL WILLIAMS
ALLEN J. SMITH

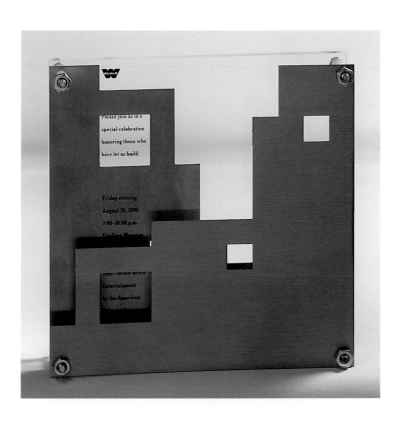

Please join us in a
special celebration
honoring those who
have let us build.

Friday evening
August 10, 1990
7:00–10:00 p.m.
Frost Art Museum

Semi-formal attire
Entertainment
by the American

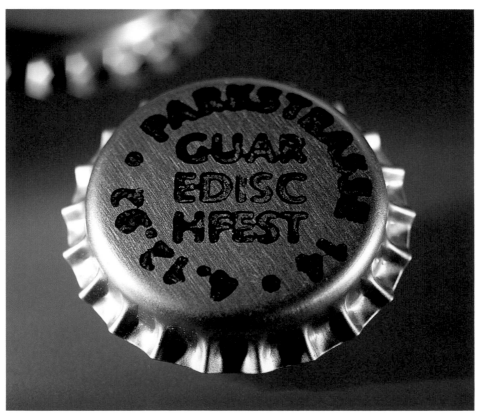

(TOP) ART DIRECTORS: MICHAEL MCGINN, TAKAAKI MATSUMOTO DESIGNER: MICHAEL MCGINN AGENCY: M
PLUS M INCORPORATED CLIENT: INDEPENDENT CURATORS INCORPORATED COUNTRY: USA
□ (BOTTOM) ART DIRECTOR/DESIGNER: FONS M. HICKMANN CLIENT: GUAREDISCH I. COUNTRY: GERMANY

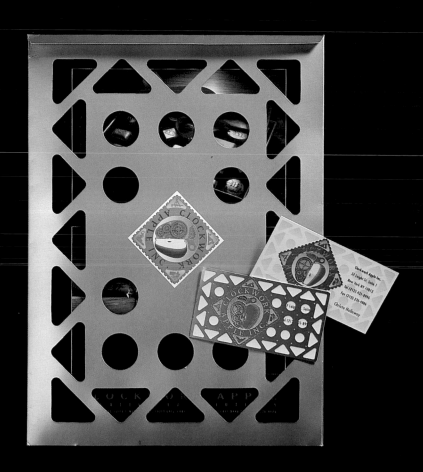

(THIS PAGE TOP) DESIGNERS: MICHAEL GAIS, THOMAS HAGENBUCHER, THEKLA HALBACH, IRIS UTIKAL

CLIENT: FACHHOCHSCHULE DÜSSELDORF COUNTRY: GERMANY □ (THIS PAGE BOTTOM)

DESIGNER: CHRISTO HOLLOWAY AGENCY: CLOCKWORK APPLE, INC. COUNTRY: USA

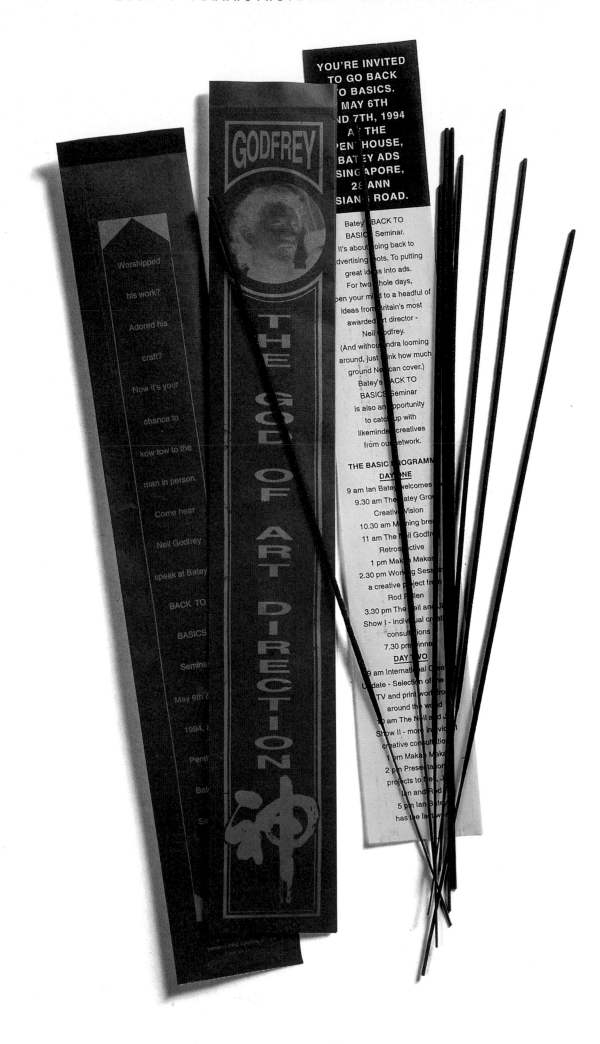

PHILIPPE LUDON / LIBRAIRIE DENISE WEIL
DIDIER LECOINTRE - DENIS OZANNE

RELIURES
LETTRISTES

AMARGER BROUTIN CANAL CARAVEN
DEVAUX DUPONT HACHETTE
DELATOUR LEMAÎTRE ISOU LETAILLEUR
LEONCINI MULLER POYET RICHOL
ROEHMER SABATIER SATIÉ SPACAGNA

VERNISSAGE

LE JEUDI 21 MARS 1991 A 18 HEURES
A LA LIBRAIRIE LECOINTRE-OZANNE
9, RUE DE TOURNON PARIS 6ème
TEL (1) 43 26 02 92

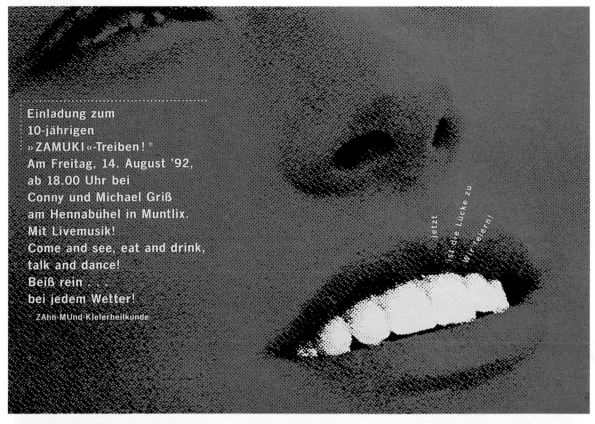

Einladung zum
10-jährigen
»ZAMUKI«-Treiben! *
Am Freitag, 14. August '92,
ab 18.00 Uhr bei
Conny und Michael Griß
am Hennabühel in Muntlix.
Mit Livemusik!
Come and see, eat and drink,
talk and dance!
Beiß rein . . .
bei jedem Wetter!
* ZAhn-MUnd-KIeferheilkunde

Jetzt
ist die Lücke zu.
Wir feiern!

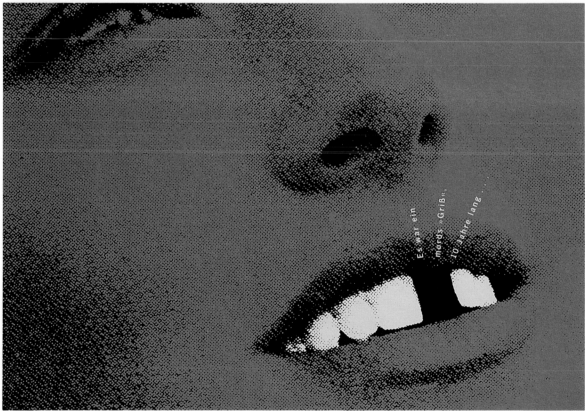

Es war ein
mords »Griß«,
10 Jahre lang . . . .

(OPPOSITE) ART DIRECTOR/DESIGNER/ILLUSTRATOR: THOMAS G. FOWLER AGENCY/CLIENT: TOM FOWLER, INC. COUNTRY: USA □ (THIS PAGE) ART DIRECTOR/DESIGNER: PETER FELDER AGENCY: FELDER GRAFIK DESIGN CLIENT: DR. MICHAEL GRISS COUNTRY: AUSTRIA

2. AUTOREN-READER

MICHAEL KLAUS

JOHN LINTHICUM

HELGA LIPPELT

INGE MEYER-DIETRICH

CLAUDIA PÜTZ

JUTTA RICHTER

SCHREIBEN LESEN HÖREN

LINDE ROTTA

DIETMAR SOUS

HALIT ÜNAL

NAMEN REZENSIONEN WERKE

(OPPOSITE) ART DIRECTOR/DESIGNER: LUTZ MENZE PHOTOGRAPHER: CICO HEUKAMP AGENCY: LUTZ MENZE DESIGN CLIENT: SEKRETARIAT FÜR GEMEINSAME KULTURARBEIT IN NRW COUNTRY: GERMANY □ (THIS PAGE TOP) CREATIVE DIRECTORS: KENT HUNTER, DANNY ABELSON DESIGNERS: STEVEN FABRIZIO, GINA STONE PHOTOGRAPHER: HANS NELEMAN AND STOCK AGENCY: FRANKFURT BALKIND PARTNERS CLIENT: AMERICAN MOVIE CLASSICS COUNTRY: USA □ (BOTTOM) ART DIRECTOR/DESIGNER: SARA ROTMAN CLIENT: SONY MUSIC ENTERTAINMENT INC. COUNTRY: USA

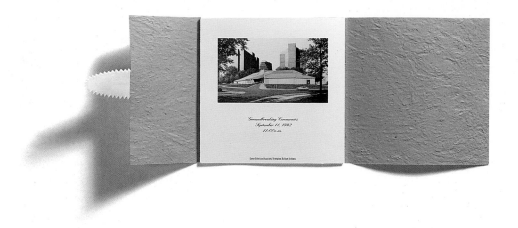

(OPPOSITE) ART DIRECTORS: STEVEN SIKORA, LYNETTE ERICKSON-SIKORA DESIGNERS: BRUCE MACINDOE, STEVEN SIKORA AGENCY:

DESIGN GUYS CLIENT: MINNESOTA PUBLIC RADIO COUNTRY: USA □ (THIS PAGE) ART DIRECTOR: JOHN MULLER DESIGNER:

SAL COSTELL PHOTOGRAPHER: STEVE CURTIS AGENCY: MULLER + COMPANY CLIENT: KANSAS CITY ART INSTITUTE COUNTRY: USA

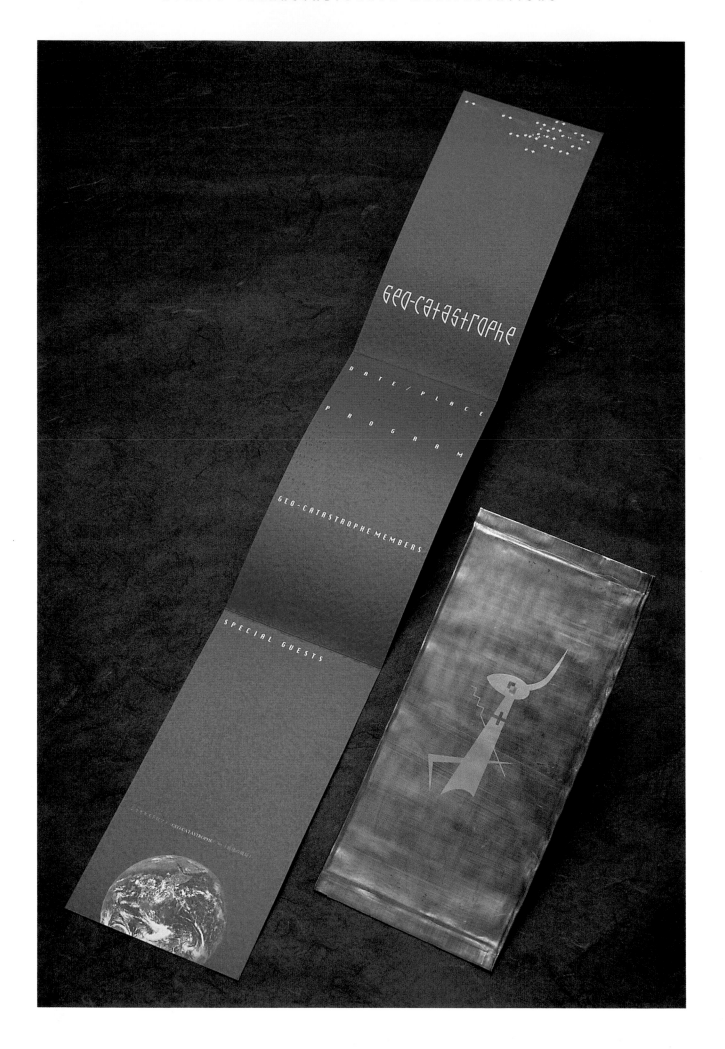

(THIS SPREAD) ART DIRECTOR: MASAYUKI SHIMIZU DESIGNERS: MASAYUKI SHIMIZU, NIO KIMURA PHOTOGRAPHER: KATUZI NISIKAWA

AGENCY: CN CORPORATION CLIENT: OSAKA GAS RESEARCH INSTITUTE FOR CULTURE, ENERGY AND LIFE (CEL) COUNTRY: JAPAN

(ABOVE LEFT) ART DIRECTOR/DESIGNER: SAM KUO STUDIO/CLIENT: KUO DESIGN OFFICE COUNTRY: USA □ (ABOVE RIGHT) ART DIRECTOR/DESIGNER: VALERIE WONG ASSISTANT DESIGNER: CARY CHIAO PHOTOGRAPHER: TOM LANDECKER AGENCY: THE DESIGN OFFICE OF WONG & YEO CLIENT: KATE FOLEY COMPANY COUNTRY: USA □ (ABOVE BOTTOM) ART DIRECTOR/DESIGNER: DOUG TRAPP COPYWRITER: CORINNE MITCHELL AGENCY: McCOOL & COMPANY CLIENT: BARRY McCOOL COUNTRY: USA □ (OPPOSITE) ART DIRECTOR: ROBERT PETRICK DESIGNER: LAURA RESS PHOTOGRAPHER: FRANÇOIS ROBERT AGENCY: PETRICK DESIGN CLIENT: DIFFA (DESIGN INDUSTRY FOUNDATION FIGHTING AIDS) COUNTRY: USA

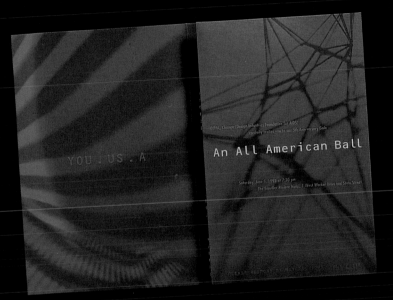

YOU

OUR STRENGTH IS OU

YOU . US . A

(DIFFA) Chicago (Design Industries Foundation For AIDS)
cordially invites you to its 5th Anniversary Gala

An All American Ball

Saturday, June 5, 1993 at 7:30 pm
The Stouffer Riviere Hotel, 1 West Wacker Drive and State Street

PLEASE RESPOND BY

DIFFA/Chicago
885F Merchandise Mart
Chicago, IL 60654

YOU

R UNITY OF PURPOSE

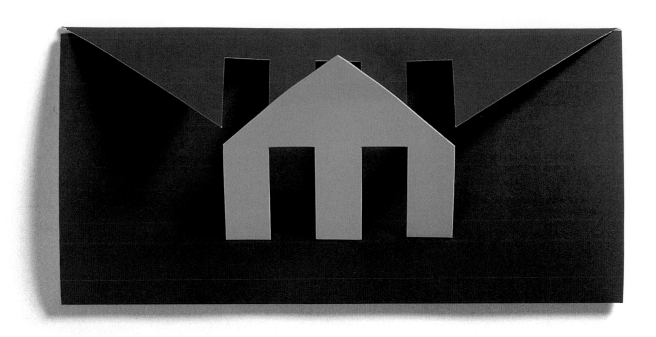

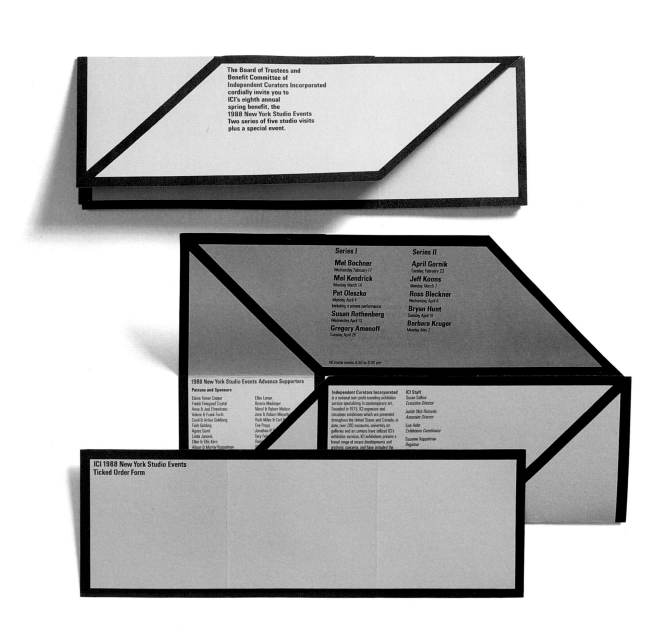

The Board of Trustees and
Benefit Committee of
Independent Curators Incorporated
cordially invite you to
ICI's eighth annual
spring benefit, the
1988 New York Studio Events
Two series of five studio visits
plus a special event.

Series I

Mel Bochner
Wednesday, February 17

Mel Kendrick
Monday, March 14

Pat Oleszko
Monday, April 4
including a private performance

Susan Rothenberg
Wednesday, April 13

Gregory Amenoff
Tuesday, April 26

Series II

April Gornik
Tuesday, February 23

Jeff Koons
Monday, March 7

Ross Bleckner
Wednesday, April 6

Bryan Hunt
Tuesday, April 19

Barbara Kruger
Monday, May 2

All studio events 6:30 to 8:30 pm

1988 New York Studio Events Advance Supporters

Patrons and Sponsors

Elaine Terner Cooper
Freddi Finegood Crystal
Anne & Joel Ehrenkranz
Valerie & Frank Furth
Carol & Arthur Goldberg
Faith Golding
Agnes Gund
Linda Janovic
Ellen & Ellis Kern
Alison & Murray Koppelman

Ellen Liman
Beatrix Medinger
Meryl & Robert Meltzer
Jane & Robert Meyerhoff
Ruth Miles & Carl
Eve Propp
Jonathan P.
Tacy Feit
Rose

Independent Curators Incorporated
is a national non-profit traveling exhibition
service specializing in contemporary art.
Founded in 1975, ICI organizes and
circulates exhibitions which are presented
throughout the United States and Canada, to
date, over 200 museums, university art
galleries and art centers have utilized ICI's
exhibition services. ICI exhibitions present a
broad range of recent developments and
aesthetic concerns, and have included the

ICI Staff
Susan Sollins
Executive Director

Judith Olch Richards
Associate Director

Lise Holst
Exhibitions Coordinator

Suzanne Koppelman
Registrar

ICI 1988 New York Studio Events
Ticked Order Form

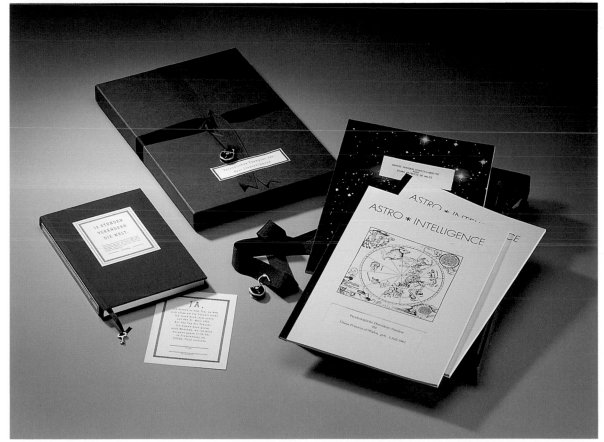

(OPPOSITE PAGE TOP) ART DIRECTOR: HEIKE JANSEN DESIGNERS: HEIKE JANSEN, MICHAEL MARSCHALL CLIENT: DEUTSCHE BANK BAUSPAR AG COUNTRY: GERMANY □ (OPPOSITE PAGE BOTTOM) ART DIRECTORS: MICHAEL MCGINN, TAKAAKI MATSUMOTO DESIGNER: MICHAEL MCGINN AGENCY: M PLUS M INCORPORATED CLIENT: INDEPENDENT CURATORS INC. COUNTRY: USA □ (THIS PAGE TOP LEFT) ART DIRECTOR: JAMES WAI MO LEUNG DESIGNER: JAMES WAI MO LEUNG AGENCY: JAMES LEUNG DESIGN CLIENT: HELGA KOPPERL COUNTRY: USA □ (THIS PAGE TOP RIGHT) ART DIRECTOR: WOLFGANG HASLINGER DESIGNER: WOLFGANG HASLINGER ILLUSTRATOR: WOLFGANG HASLINGER CLIENT: BZW-WERBEAGENTUR COUNTRY: AUSTRIA □ (THIS PAGE BOTTOM) ART DIRECTOR: DESIGNER: SUSANNE AHLERS AGENCY: RG WIESMEIER WERBEAGENTUR GMBH CLIENT: OP COUTURE BRILLEN GMBH COUNTRY: GERMANY

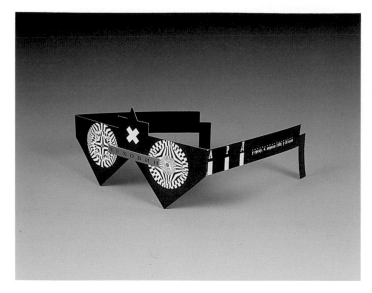

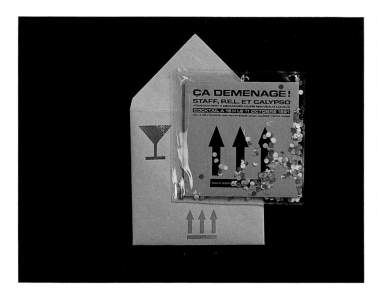

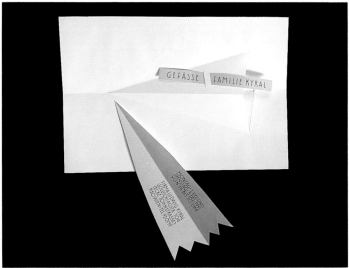

(THIS PAGE TOP LEFT) ART DIRECTOR/DESIGNER: EDUARD CEHOVIN CLIENT: EDUARD CEHOVIN COUNTRY: SLOVENIA □ (THIS PAGE TOP RIGHT) ART DIRECTOR: ANTONIO ROMANO PHOTOGRAPHER: GIUSEPPE MARIA FADDA AGENCY: AR&A ANTONIO ROMANO & ASSOCIATI CLIENT: FINMECCANICA COUNTRY: ITALY □ (ABOVE CENTER) ART DIRECTOR/DESIGNER: DAGMAR SCHROEBLER AGENCY: RG WIESMEIER WERBEAGENTUR GMBH CLIENT: PANAMA JACK COUNTRY: SPAIN □ (ABOVE BOTTOM LEFT) ART DIRECTORS: JÉRÔME OUDIN, SUSANNA SHANNON DESIGNERS: JÉRÔME OUDIN, SUSANNA SHANNON AGENCY: DESIGN DEPT. CLIENT: STAFF P.E.L. ET CALYPSO COUNTRY: FRANCE □ (THIS PAGE BOTTOM RIGHT) ART DIRECTOR/DESIGNER: VERONIKA KYRAL AGENCY: VERONIKA KYRAL CLIENT: FA. LUDWIG KYRAL COUNTRY: AUSTRIA

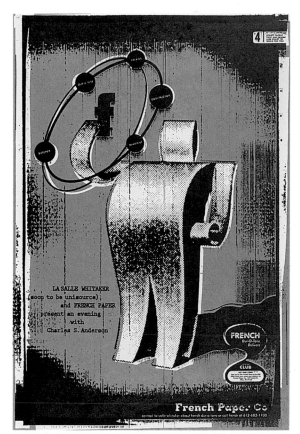

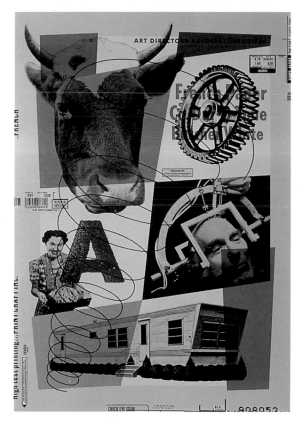

(ALL IMAGES THIS PAGE) ART DIRECTOR: CHARLES S. ANDERSON AGENCY: CHARLES S. ANDERSON DESIGN CO. □ (THIS PAGE TOP LEFT) DESIGNERS: CHARLES S. ANDERSON, JOEL TEMPLIN CLIENT: LASALLE WHITAKER COUNTRY: USA □ (THIS PAGE TOP RIGHT) DESIGNERS: CHARLES S. ANDERSON, PAUL HOWART PHOTOGRAPHER: DARRELL EAGER CLIENT: AMERICAN CENTER FOR DESIGN COUNTRY: USA □ (THIS PAGE BOTTOM LEFT) DESIGNERS: CHARLES S. ANDERSON, TODD HAUSWIRTH CLIENT: ART DIRECTORS ASSOCIATION OF IOWA COUNTRY: USA □ (THIS PAGE BOTTOM RIGHT) DESIGNERS: CHARLES S. ANDERSON, TODD HAUSWIRTH CLIENT: AIGA LOS ANGELES COUNTRY: USA

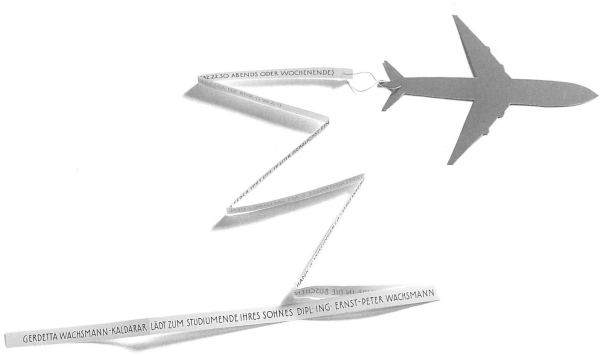

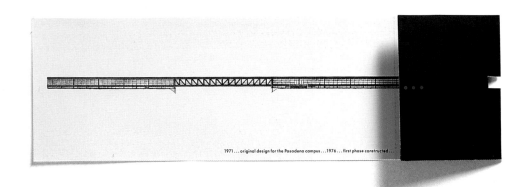

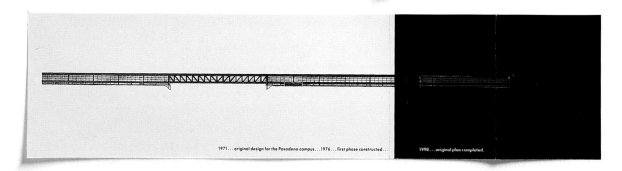

(ABOVE TOP) ART DIRECTOR/DESIGNER/ILLUSTRATOR/AGENCY: VERONIKA KYRAL CLIENT: WACHSMANN COUNTRY: AUSTRIA □ (ABOVE BOTTOM) ART DIRECTOR: REBECA MENDEZ DESIGNER: SZE TSUNG LEONG AGENCY: ART CENTER COLLEGE OF DESIGN OFFICE CLIENT: ART CENTER COLLEGE OF DESIGN COUNTRY: USA □ (OPPOSITE) ART DIRECTOR: KIT HINRICHS DESIGNER: MARK SELFE PHOTOGRAPHER: BARRY ROBINSON ART: KIT HINRICHS AGENCY: PENTAGRAM DESIGN CLIENTS: SAN FRANCISCO MOMA, SAN FRANCISCO ARCHITECTURAL FOUNDATION, MUSEUM ARTS COUNCIL COUNTRY: USA

The Modern Art Council of the
San Francisco Museum of Modern Art
401 Van Ness Avenue,
San Francisco, California 94102-4582

**BEAUX
ARTS
BALL
1993**

AN INVITATION
A benefit for the SFMOMA
Department of Architecture and Design

The American Institute of Architects
San Francisco Chapter
The Architectural Foundation of San Francisco
The Modern Art Council of the
San Francisco Museum of Modern Art
cordially invite you to attend the

BEAUX ARTS BALL 1993

...ay, April 21, 1993
...tt San Francisco
...al Reserve Building
...ween Sacramento and Clay

...igning of Museum Girder
... Dinner
...e, judging, and prizes
...table centerpieces closes
...est table design

...by

...Tie

...sponsors, the
...sier Corporation
...ncisco

Join 40 of San Francisco's
top architects and designers for dinner and
costume ball to celebrate the "Topping Out"
and completion of the structure of the San Francisco
Museum of Modern Art's new building.

WEST THAMES COLLEGE DIPLOMA SHOW. ADVERTISING & GRAPHIC DESIGN: Villa Carlotta 39 Charlotte St. W1.
Tuesday 21 June Private View 6-9. Open to the public Wednesday 22 June 10-5.30 RSVP 081 568 0244 x 217.

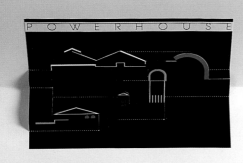

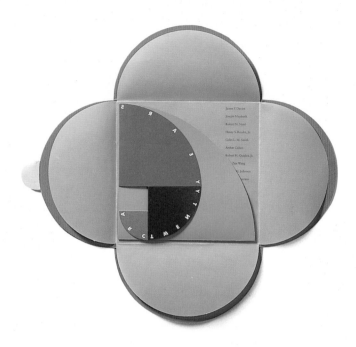

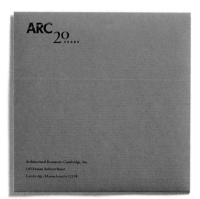

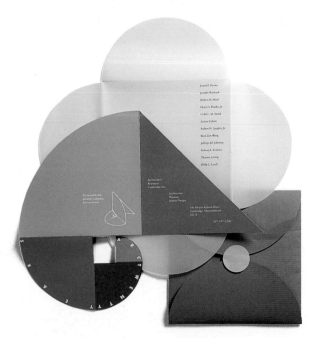

(OPPOSITE TOP) ART DIRECTOR/DESIGNER/COPYWRITER: MICHAEL McPHERSON AGENCY: COREY McPHERSON NASH CLIENT: ARCHI-TECTURAL RESOURCES CAMBRIDGE COUNTRY: USA □ (OPPOSITE CENTER) ART DIRECTOR/DESIGNER: JOHN SPATCHURST AGENCY: SPATCHURST DESIGN ASSOC. CLIENT: ART GALLERY OF NEW SOUTH WALES COUNTRY: AUSTRALIA □ (OPPOSITE BOTTOM) ART DIRECTOR/DESIGNER: COLIN JAMES ROWAN ILLUSTRATOR: EMERY VINCENT ASSOC. AGENCY: JANE SILVER SMITH CLIENT: MINISTRY OF THE ARTS COUNTRY: AUSTRALIA □ (ABOVE) ART DIRECTOR: VINCENT McEVOY DESIGNER: VINCENT McEVOY PHOTOGRAPHER: ALISTAIR OGILVIE CLIENT: WEST THAMES COLLEGE COUNTRY: GREAT BRITAIN

AWARDS PROGRAM

Vážený spoluobčane! Posíláme Vám na ukázku tzv. *malířský klínek,* nezbytnou součást moderních tendencí v malířství nejen XX. století. Klínky tohoto či téměř shodného tvaru používali mistři palety a štětce, jejichž jména čítáme v těch nejnedostupnějších katalozích, stejně jako ti, jejichž jména v týchž katalozích postrádáme, jimiž se ale hemží katalogy zbytečné a nezajímavé. Klínků shodných s tímto vzorkem užívá rovněž mladá malířka **IRENA WAGNEROVÁ**, o čemž se můžete přesvědčit na její 4. samostatné výstavě, pořádané Aktivem mladých výtvarníků ve spolupráci s SČVU, **v Galerii mladých** (U Řečických) v Praze 1, Vodičkově ulici 10, ve dnech od 25. října do 5. listopadu 1989, nejlépe však při slavnostním zahájení **25. října v 17 hodin**. Hostem Ireny Wagnerové je malířka **Dorota Zlatohlávková**. Výstava je otevřena denně mimo pondělí v 10–13 a v 14–18 hodin. Těšíme se na Vaši návštěvu.

Klínek, tzv. *malířský*

Ukázka praktického *použití klínku* v případě Ireny Wagnerové:

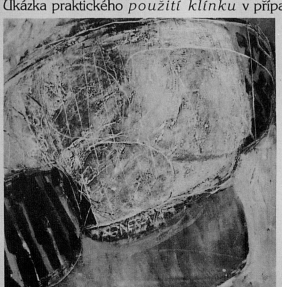

Na obraze z cyklu „Kameny a mušle" (olej, 1988, 29 ½ × 29 ½") není klínek zpředu vidět,... ale detail zadní strany obrazu hovoří jasně!

(OPPOSITE) ART DIRECTOR/DESIGNER: PAVEL BENES PHOTOGRAPHERS: JAN SILPOCH, W.C. CULVER AGENCY: GRAPHIC DESIGN PAVEL BENES CLIENT: IRENA WAGNEROVA COUNTRY: CZECH REPUBLIC □ (ABOVE) ART DIRECTORS: MICHAEL MCGINN, TAKAAKI MATSUMOTO DESIGNER: MICHAEL MCGINN AGENCY: M PLUS M INC. CLIENT: INDEPENDENT CURATORS INC. COUNTRY: USA

HERRON GALLERY
Indianapolis Center for Contemporary Art
CLAYFEST No. 8
A Juried Biennial of
INDIANA CERAMIC ARTISTS
and
AMACO SELECTS: TEN YEARS OF CERAMIC WORKSHOPS

DECEMBER 5, 1992 - JANUARY 8, 1993

HERRON SCHOOL OF ART
1701 N. PENNSYLVANIA ST.
INDIANAPOLIS, IN. 46202
317 920-2420

MONDAY - THURSDAY
10:00 AM TO 7:00 PM
FRIDAY 10:00 AM TO 5:00 PM

These exhibitions are funded in part by The Mary Howes
Woodsmall Foundation, American Art Clay Co., Inc., the Friends
of Herron, the Indiana Arts Commission and the National
Endowment for the Arts.

(ABOVE) DESIGNER: JIM ROSS AGENCY: MIRELEZ/ROSS CLIENT: HERRON GALLERY COUNTRY: USA □ (OPPOSITE) ART DIRECTOR/
DESIGNER: AMY MCFARLAND PHOTOGRAPHER: BARBARA LYTER CLIENT: LOS ANGELES COUNTY MUSEUM OF ART COUNTRY: USA

When Art Became Fashion:
KOSODE IN EDO-PERIOD JAPAN

—— I/We accept the invitation for:
Wednesday evening, November 11, 1992.

—— I/We regret.

_____
Please print name(s)

A dynamic urban culture flourished
in Edo-period Japan (1615–1868),
leaving a legacy of plays and novels,
woodblock prints, and extraordinary designs on clothing. An escape
from mundane concerns was provided by the kabuki theaters and
pleasure quarters of the "floating
world," where actors and highly
refined courtesans set fashion for all
levels of society.

The primary garment of both
men and women in Edo-period Japan
was the kosode, predecessor of the
modern kimono. The kosode, the
graphic potential of which was

exploited by highly skilled artisans,
became a "canvas" moving in three-
dimensional space. Possessing a com-
plex integration of design and form,
the often elaborately decorated
kosode expressed the same aesthetic
characteristics that infused all the
arts produced under the rule of the
Tokugawa shogunate. More than
two hundred works, including
kosode, obi, genre paintings, and
woodblock-printed pattern books,
shown in two rotations, represent
this flowering of the textile arts
of Japan.

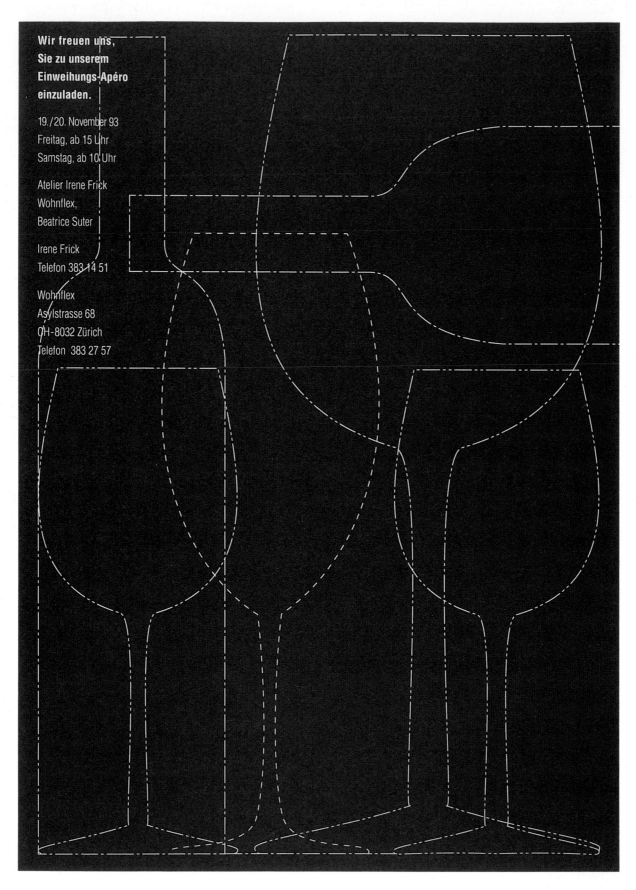

**Wir freuen uns,
Sie zu unserem
Einweihungs-Apéro
einzuladen.**

19./20. November 93
Freitag, ab 15 Uhr
Samstag, ab 10 Uhr

Atelier Irene Frick
Wohnflex,
Beatrice Suter

Irene Frick
Telefon 383 14 51

Wohnflex
Asylstrasse 68
CH-8032 Zürich
Telefon 383 27 57

(THIS PAGE) ART DIRECTOR/DESIGNER/ILLUSTRATOR/AGENCY: BBV PROF. MICHAEL BAVIERA CLIENT: WOHNFLEX ZÜRICH
COUNTRY: SWITZERLAND □ (OPPOSITE PAGE) ART DIRECTOR: JENNIFER MORLA DESIGNERS: JENNIFER MORLA,
CRAIG BAILEY PHOTOGRAPHER: MAN RAY AGENCY: MORLA DESIGN CLIENT: AIGA/LA COUNTRY: USA

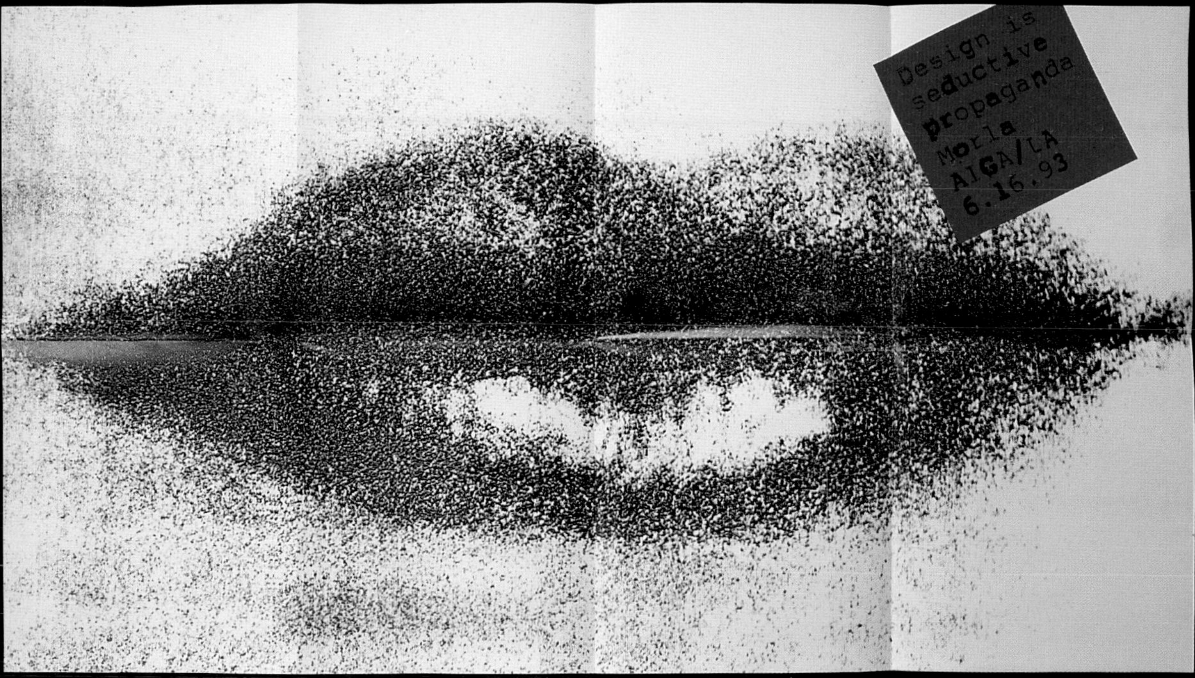

Design is
seductive
propaganda
Morla
AIGA/LA
6.16.93

A. *Jonathan Combs*
  Scratchboard & airbrush

B. *Bill Cannon*
  Photograph

C. *David Harto*
  Airbrush ink & gouache

D. *Kathlyn Shadle*
  Scratchboard & dyes

E. *Chuck Pyle*
  Oil

F. *Steve Coppin*
  Airbrush ink

G. *Vikki Leib*
  Computer

H. *Larry Duke*
  Scratchboard & watercolor

I. *John C. Smith*
  Computer

J. *Bobbi Tull*
  Watercolor

K. *Elizabeth Read*
  Scratchboard & watercolor

L. *Dennis Orchner*
  Colored pencil

M. *Bruce Morser*
  Pencil

(OPPOSITE) ART DIRECTOR/DESIGNER: KEISUKE UNOSAWA AGENCY/CLIENT: KEISUKE UNOSAWA DESIGN COUNTRY: JAPAN □ (ABOVE) ART DIRECTORS/DESIGNERS: JANET KRUSE, TRACI DABERKO ARTISTS (FROM LEFT TO RIGHT): JONATHAN COMBS, BILL CANNON, DAVID HARTO AGENCY: THE LEONHARDT GROUP CLIENT: PAT HACKETT ARTIST REPRESENTATIVE COUNTRY: USA

(ABOVE) ART DIRECTOR: JARED SCHNEIDMAN DESIGNER: GUILBERT GATES ILLUSTRATORS: JARED SCHNEIDMAN, GUILBERT GATES, KATHLEEN KATIMS AGENCY: JARED SCHNEIDMAN DESIGN COUNTRY: USA □ (OPPOSITE PAGE TOP) ART DIRECTORS: STEVEN JINEL, FRÉDÉRIC BOSSER DESIGNER: STEVEN JINEL AGENCY: CAPONE CLIENT: ETUDE BOISGIRARD COUNTRY: FRANCE □ (OPPOSITE PAGE BOTTOM) ILLUSTRATOR: ERHARD HÖNICKE COUNTRY: SWITZERLAND

(ABOVE) ART DIRECTOR: FRITZ W. WURSTER DESIGNERS: SABINE RENNER, LESLIE SPEER PHOTOGRAPHERS: JENS WERLEIN, FRITZ W. WURSTER AGENCY/CLIENT: INDUSTRIAL DESIGNERS, FRITZ W. WURSTER COUNTRY: GERMANY □ (OPPOSITE) ART DIRECTOR: STEVE TOLLESON DESIGNERS: STEVE TOLLESON, MARK WINN AGENCY: TOLLESON DESIGN CLIENT: COTTONG + TANIGUCHI COUNTRY: USA

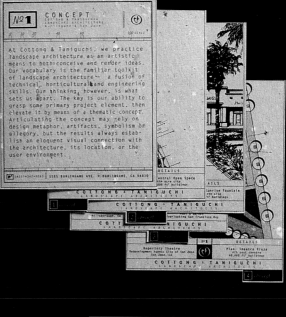

CONCEPT

Nº 1

COTTONG & TANIGUCHI
LANDSCAPE ARCHITECTURE
Burlingame & San Jose

At Cottong & Taniguchi, we practice
landscape architecture as an artistic
means to both conceive and render ideas.
Our vocabulary is the familiar toolkit
of landscape architecture — a fusion of
technical, horticultural and engineering
skills. Our thinking, however, is what
sets us apart. The key is our ability to
grasp some primary project element, then
elevate it by means of a thematic concept.
Articulating the concept may rely on
design metaphor, artifacts, symbolism or
allegory, but the results always estab-
lish an eloquent visual connection with
the architecture, its location, or the
user environment.

1105 BURLINGAME AVE, BURLINGAME, CA 94010

COTTONG & TANIGUCHI
LANDSCAPE ARCHITECTS

Nº 1 CONCEPT

RECENT PROJECTS | details

Nº 2 BALANCE

RECENT PROJECTS | details

Nº 4 STRUCTURE

RECENT PROJECTS | details

Nº 3 INTERACTION

RECENT PROJECTS | details

(OPPOSITE) ART DIRECTOR: CHARLES HIVELY DESIGNER: CHARLES HIVELY AGENCY: THE HIVELY AGENCY CLIENT:
ADMINISTAFF COUNTRY: USA □ (THIS PAGE) ART DIRECTORS: FRANCES NEWELL, JOHN SORRELL DESIGNER:
MARK-STEEN ADAMSON AGENCY: NEWELL AND SORRELL CLIENT: UNION RAILWAYS LIMITED COUNTRY: GREAT BRITAIN

(THIS PAGE) ART DIRECTOR: VICKIE SCHAFER DESIGNER: VICKIE SCHAFER PHOTOGRAPHER: CAROL KAPLAN STUDIO AGENCY: SIQUIS, LTD. CLIENT: THE SCHWAB COMPANY COUNTRY: USA □ (OPPOSITE PAGE) ART DIRECTOR/DESIGNER: CHRISTO HOLLOWAY PHOTOGRAPHER: RICK BURDA AGENCY: CLOCKWORK APPLE, INC. CLIENT: MTV COUNTRY: USA

(Opposite) Art Director/Copywriter: CLARE ULTIMO Designer: JULIE HUBNER Agency/Client: ULTIMO INC. Country: USA

☐ (Above) Art Directors: ANTONY REDMAN, THAM KHAI MENG Designers: ANTONY REDMAN, THAM KHAI MENG

Agency: BATEY ADS SINGAPORE Clients: BATEY ADS SINGAPORE, SINGAPORE AIRLINES Country: SINGAPORE

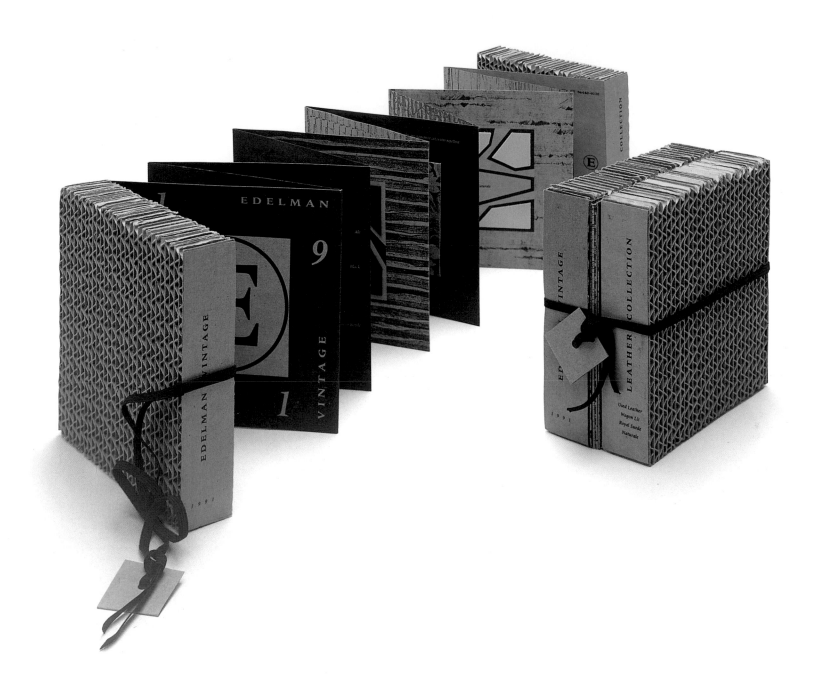

(ABOVE) CREATIVE DIRECTOR/ART DIRECTOR/DESIGNER: MAY LIU COPYWRITER: TEDDY EDELMAN CLIENT: TEDDY & ARTHUR EDELMAN, LTD. COUNTRY: USA □ (OPPOSITE TOP LEFT) ART DIRECTOR: RACHEL MANDEL DESIGNER/ILLUSTRATOR: TRACY SABIN AGENCY: TRACY SABIN GRAPHIC DESIGN CLIENT: HORTON PLAZA COUNTRY: USA □ (TOP RIGHT) ART DIRECTOR: DENNIS ERBER DESIGNER: THOMAS RENK CLIENT: THOMSON C.E. COUNTRY: USA □ (BOTTOM LEFT) ART DIRECTOR: ALAN CHAN DESIGNERS: ALAN CHAN, PETER LO AGENCY: ALAN CHAN DESIGN COMPANY CLIENT: MR. CHAN TEA ROOM LTD. COUNTRY: HONG KONG □ (BOTTOM RIGHT) ART DIRECTOR: CHARLES S. ANDERSON DESIGNERS/ILLUSTRATORS: CHARLES S. ANDERSON, PAUL HOWART AGENCY: CHARLES S. ANDERSON DESIGN CO. CLIENT: TURNER CLASSIC MOVIES COUNTRY: USA

(OPPOSITE) ART DIRECTOR/DESIGNER: ERICH FALKNER COPYWRITER: DR. ANDREAS HOCHSTÖGER AGENCY: GGK WIEN
WERBEAGENTUR CLIENT: PORSCHE AUSTRIA GESMBH & CO COUNTRY: AUSTRIA □ (ABOVE TOP) ART DIRECTOR/
DESIGNER: JOHN SWIETER PHOTOGRAPHERS: MAX WEISS AGENCY: SWIETER DESIGN CLIENT: YOUNG PRESIDENTS'
ORGANIZATION COUNTRY: USA □ (BOTTOM) ART DIRECTOR: THOMAS G. FOWLER DESIGNERS: THOMAS G. FOWLER,
KARL S. MARUYAMA PHOTOGRAPHER: RANDY DUCHAINE AGENCY: TOM FOWLER, INC. CLIENT: H.T. WOODS COUNTRY: USA

(OPPOSITE TOP) ART DIRECTOR: STEFAN OEVERMANN DESIGNER: MARIE-LUISE DORST PHOTOGRAPHER: WALTER SCHELS ILLUSTRATOR:
THOMAS WOBER AGENCY: RG WIESMEIER WERBEAGENTUR CLIENT: CONVATEC BRISTOL-MYERS COUNTRY: GERMANY □
(OPPOSITE BOTTOM AND THIS PAGE) ART DIRECTOR: ALAN CHAN DESIGNERS: ALAN CHAN, CHEN SHUN TSOI ILLUSTRATOR:
ALAN CRACKNEL AGENCY: ALAN CHAN DESIGN CLIENT: MANDARIAN ORIENTAL HK, THE FLOWER SHOP COUNTRY: HONG KONG

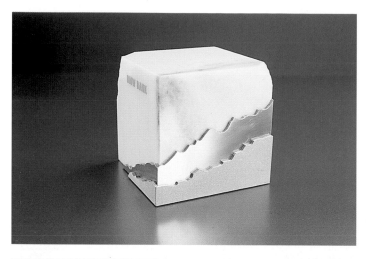

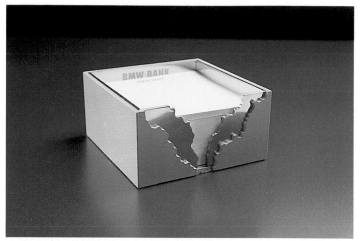

(THIS PAGE TOP) ART DIRECTOR: HERIBERT DANKL DESIGNER: HERIBERT DANKL AGENCY: ADWERBA CLIENT: BMW AUSTRIA BANK COUNTRY: AUSTRIA □ (THIS PAGE BOTTOM LEFT) ART DIRECTOR: WOLFGANG HASLINGER DESIGNER: WOLFGANG HASLINGER COUNTRY: AUSTRIA □ (THIS PAGE BOTTOM RIGHT) ART DIRECTOR: JAC COVERDALE DESIGNER: JAC COVERDALE AGENCY: CLARITY COVERDALE FURY ADVERTISING, INC. CLIENT: NORTHWESTERN NATIONAL LIFE COUNTRY: USA □ (OPPOSITE PAGE) ART DIRECTOR: STEVE WEDEEN DESIGNER: STEVE WEDEEN ILLUSTRATORS: STEVE WEDEEN, CHIP WYLY AGENCY: VAUGHN WEDEEN CREATIVE CLIENT: US WEST COMMUNICATIONS COUNTRY: USA

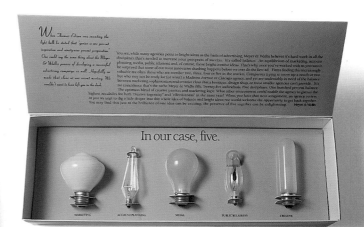

(ABOVE) CREATIVE DIRECTOR: TIM WALLIS ART DIRECTOR: TERRY KRALL COPYWRITER: TIM WALLIS PRODUCER: JULES MILLER AGENCY: MEYER & WALLIS CLIENT: MEYER & WALLIS COUNTRY: USA □ (OPPOSITE) ART DIRECTOR: MARK JOHNSON COPYWRITER: JOHN STINGLEY AGENCY: FALLON MCELLIGOTT CLIENT: FALLON MCELLIGOTT COUNTRY: USA

We wouldn't want to lose our favorite client, so we painstakingly selected this fine French bubbly as a gift for our friends at Porsche.

Drive carefully this holiday season.

From all of us at Fallon McElligott.

Umzug

Büro X
Karina Bednorz
Lo Breier
Gisela Buchhold
Kai Eichenauer
René von Falkenburg
Regina Hauschildt
Gaby Jakobskötter
Wigand Koch
Anne Rodenberg
Stefan Rodig
Andreas Schomberg
Jürg Scheurer
Hanno Tietgens

ab Montag, 2. März
Mittelweg 17
2000 Hamburg 13
Tel.: (040) 36 11 99
Fax.: (040) 37 80 18

Umzug

Büro X
Karina Bednorz
Lo Breier
Gisela Buchhold
Kai Eichenauer
René von Falkenburg
Regina Hauschildt
Gaby Jakobskötter
Wigand Koch
Anne Rodenberg
Stefan Rodig
Andreas Schomberg
Jürg Scheurer
Hanno Tietgens

ab Montag, 2. März
Mittelweg 17
2000 Hamburg 13
Tel.: (040) 36 11 99
Fax.: (040) 37 80 18

GRAPHIS VERLAG
ZHD. ARLETTE ZUPPINGER
DUFOURSTRASSE 107
8008 ZÜRICH

WIR SIND UMGEZOGEN.

Denk an uns

KARTE UMDREHEN. KLEBESCHUTZ-FOLIE ABZIEHEN UND
DAS RUNDE MAGNETPLÄTTCHEN ANS ARMATURENBRETT
KLEBEN. DER FOTORAHMEN KANN NUN NACH BELIEBEN
ANGEBRACHT UND WIEDER ABGENOMMEN WERDEN.

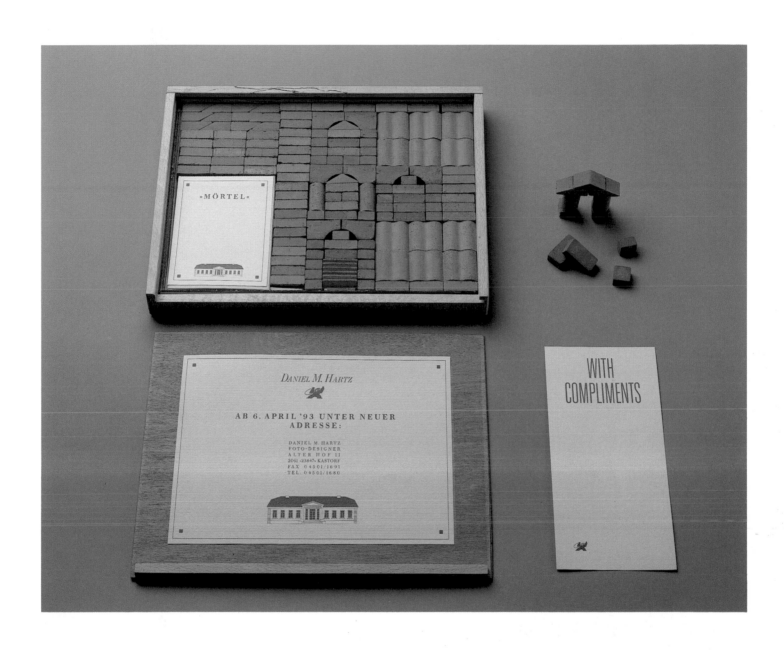

(OPPOSITE PAGE TOP) ART DIRECTOR: LO BREIER DESIGNER: JÜRG SCHEURER AGENCY/CLIENT: BÜRO X COUNTRY: GERMANY □
(OPPOSITE PAGE BOTTOM) ART DIRECTOR: MICHEL GIRARDIN DESIGNER: MICHEL GIRARDIN PHOTOGRAPHER:
STÉFANIE COUSIN AGENCY/CLIENT: BRUN UND BÜRGIN FOTOGRAFEN SWF COUNTRY: SWITZERLAND □ (THIS PAGE)
ART DIRECTOR/CLIENT: DANIEL HARTZ DESIGNER: FRANZISKA HARTZ ILLUSTRATOR: WERNER HARTZ COUNTRY: GERMANY

(TOP) ART DIRECTOR: ALBERTO BACCARI DESIGNER: TITTI SOFFIANTINO PHOTOGRAPHER: MARIO MONGE AGENCY: ARMANDO TESTA S.P.A. CLIENT: ARMANDO TESTA S.P.A. COUNTRY: ITALY □ (BOTTOM) ART DIRECTOR/DESIGNER/ILLUSTRATOR: BBV PROF. MICHAEL BAVIERA AGENCY: BBV PROF. MICHAEL BAVIERA CLIENT: J. HORBER COUNTRY: SWITZERLAND

(THIS PAGE TOP) ART DIRECTOR/DESIGNER/ILLUSTRATOR/AGENCY: BBV PROF. MICHAEL BAVIERA CLIENT: T & O TREUHAND
COUNTRY: SWITZERLAND □ (THIS PAGE CENTER) ART DIRECTOR: JIMMY YANG DESIGNER: JIMMY YANG PHOTOGRAPHER:
NAD NAIM AGENCY/CLIENT: IDENTICA COUNTRY: GREAT BRITAIN □ (THIS PAGE BOTTOM) ART DIRECTOR: ROLAND
SCHNEIDER ILLUSTRATOR: MICHAELA BAUER AGENCY: BAUERS BÜRO CLIENT: BAUERS BÜRO COUNTRY: GERMANY

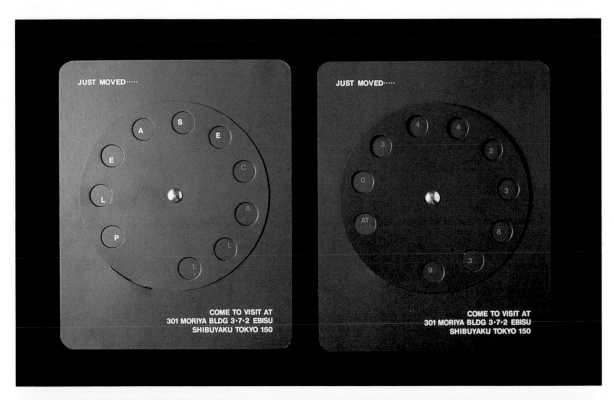

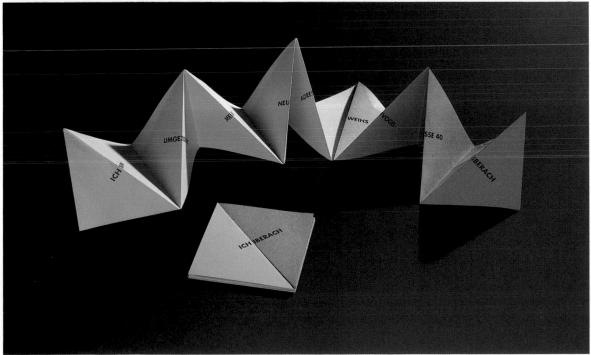

(OPPOSITE PAGE) ART DIRECTORS/DESIGNERS: SUSANNA SHANNON, JÉRÔME SAINT-LOUBERT BIÉ PHOTOGRAPHER: JÉRÔME SAINT-LOUBERT BIÉ AGENCY: DESIGN DEPT. CLIENT: IRREGULAMADAIRE COUNTRY: FRANCE □ (THIS PAGE TOP) ART DIRECTOR: KEISUKE UNOSAWA DESIGNER: KEISUKE UNOSAWA AGENCY/CLIENT: KEISUKE UNOSAWA DESIGN COUNTRY: JAPAN □ (THIS PAGE BOTTOM) DESIGNER: SASCHA WEIHS CLIENT: SASCHA WEIHS COUNTRY: GERMANY

Traslochiamo

da Foro Bonaparte, 63
a via Rugabella, 1

a Milano

STUDIO ROMANO

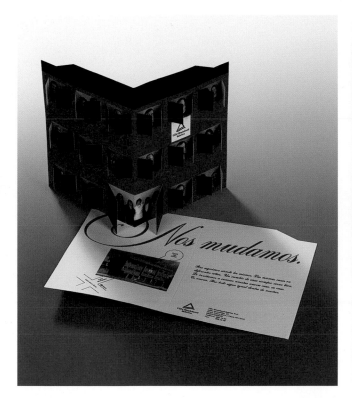

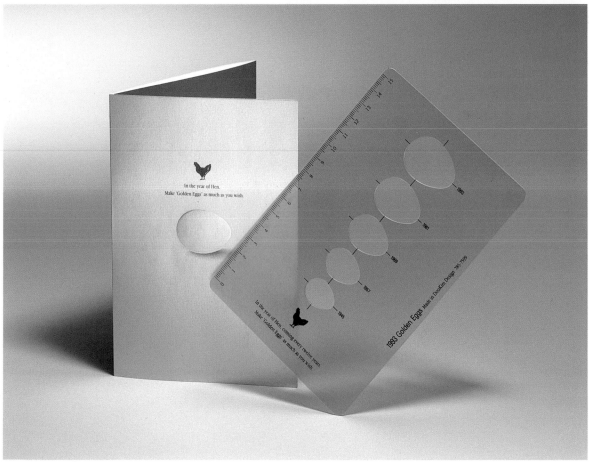

(OPPOSITE PAGE) ART DIRECTOR: ANTONIO ROMANO PHOTOGRAPHER: GIUSEPPE MARIA FADDA AGENCY/CLIENT: AR&A ANTONIO ROMANO & ASSOCIATI COUNTRY: ITALY □ (THIS PAGE TOP LEFT) ART DIRECTOR: KLAUS KRAEGE DESIGNER: KLAUS KRAEGE PHOTOGRAPHER: KLAUS KRAEGE CLIENT: TÜV RHEINLAND IBÉRICA S.A. COUNTRY: SPAIN □ (THIS PAGE TOP RIGHT) ART DIRECTOR: KENNETH KARLSSON DESIGNER: KENNETH KARLSSON ILLUSTRATOR: KENNETH KARLSSON AGENCY/CLIENT: ATELJÉ ELEFANTEN & FARET AB COUNTRY: SWEDEN □ (THIS PAGE BOTTOM) ART DIRECTOR: DOO H. KIM DESIGNERS: DONGIL LEE, JIWON SHIN AGENCY: DOOKIM DESIGN CLIENT: DOOKIM DESIGN COUNTRY: SOUTH KOREA

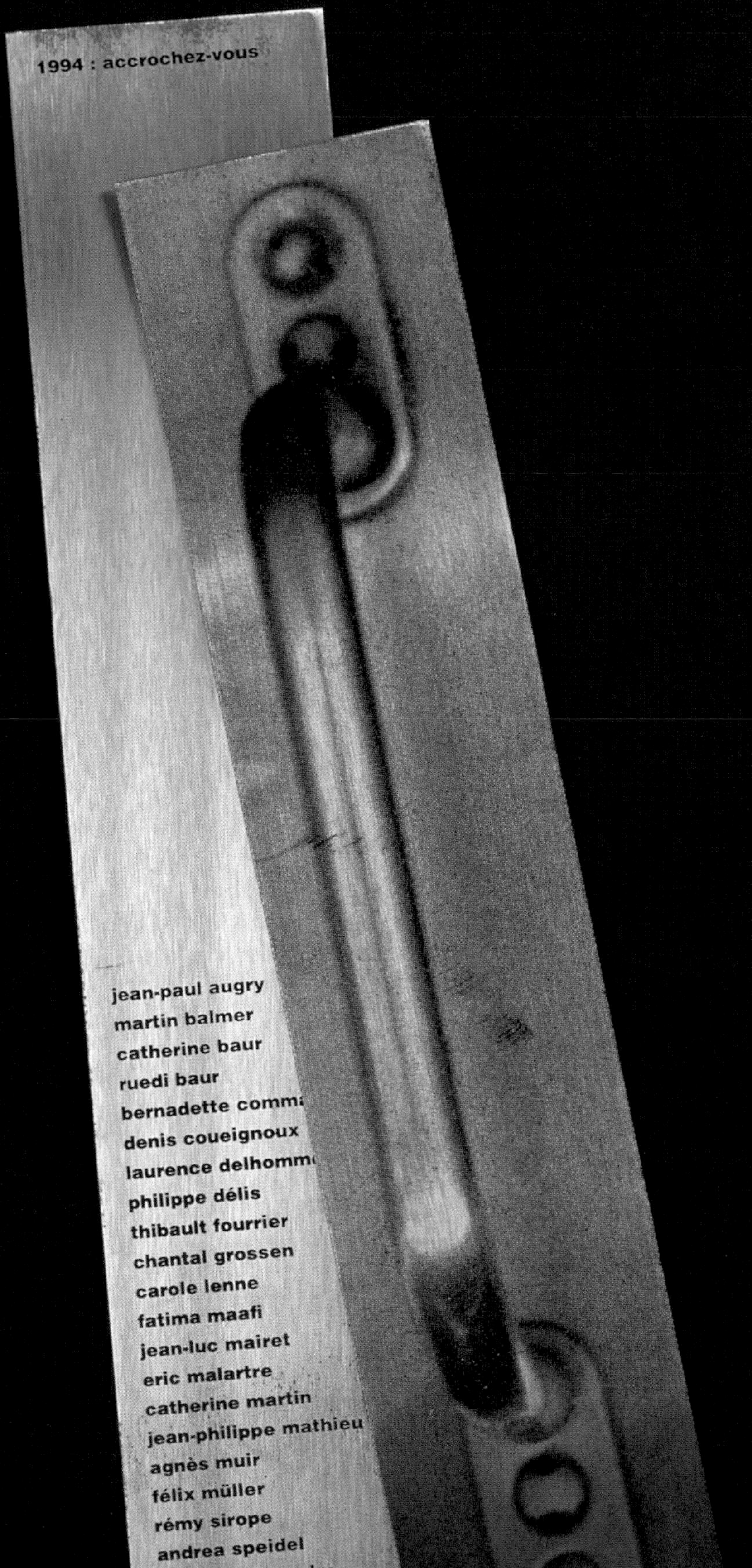

1994 : accrochez-vous

jean-paul augry
martin balmer
catherine baur
ruedi baur
bernadette comma
denis coueignoux
laurence delhomm
philippe délis
thibault fourrier
chantal grossen
carole lenne
fatima maafi
jean-luc mairet
eric malartre
catherine martin
jean-philippe mathieu
agnès muir
félix müller
rémy sirope
andrea speidel
liana yaroslavsky

DEC 31

CELEBRATE
THE BEGINNING
OF THE LAST...

DECADENCE

WILL GET
US THROUGH
THE TIMES
AHEAD.

8 O'CLOCK
AT THE GOODS
RSVP
526-2990

(OPPOSITE PAGE) DESIGNER: RUEDI BAUR AGENCY: INTÉGRAL RUEDI BAUR ET ASSOCIÉS COUNTRY: FRANCE □ (THIS PAGE) ART DIRECTOR: PETER GOOD COPYWRITER: PETER GOOD DESIGNERS: PETER GOOD, JANET GOOD, SUSAN FASICK-JONES AGENCY: PETER GOOD GRAPHIC DESIGN CLIENTS: PETER GOOD, JANET GOOD COUNTRY: USA

(THIS PAGE) ART DIRECTOR: THOMAS G. FOWLER DESIGNER: THOMAS G. FOWLER AGENCY/CLIENT: TOM FOWLER, INC.
COUNTRY: USA □ (OPPOSITE TOP) ART DIRECTOR: BRUNO K. WIESE DESIGNER: BRUNO K. WIESE STUDIO: BK WIESE
VISUAL DESIGN CLIENTS: BRUNO WIESE, RUTH WIESE COUNTRY: GERMANY □ (OPPOSITE BOTTOM) ART DIRECTOR:
ERKEN KAGAROV DESIGNER: ERKEN KAGAROV ILLUSTRATOR: ERKEN KAGAROV AGENCY/CLIENT: IMA-PRESS COUNTRY: RUSSIA

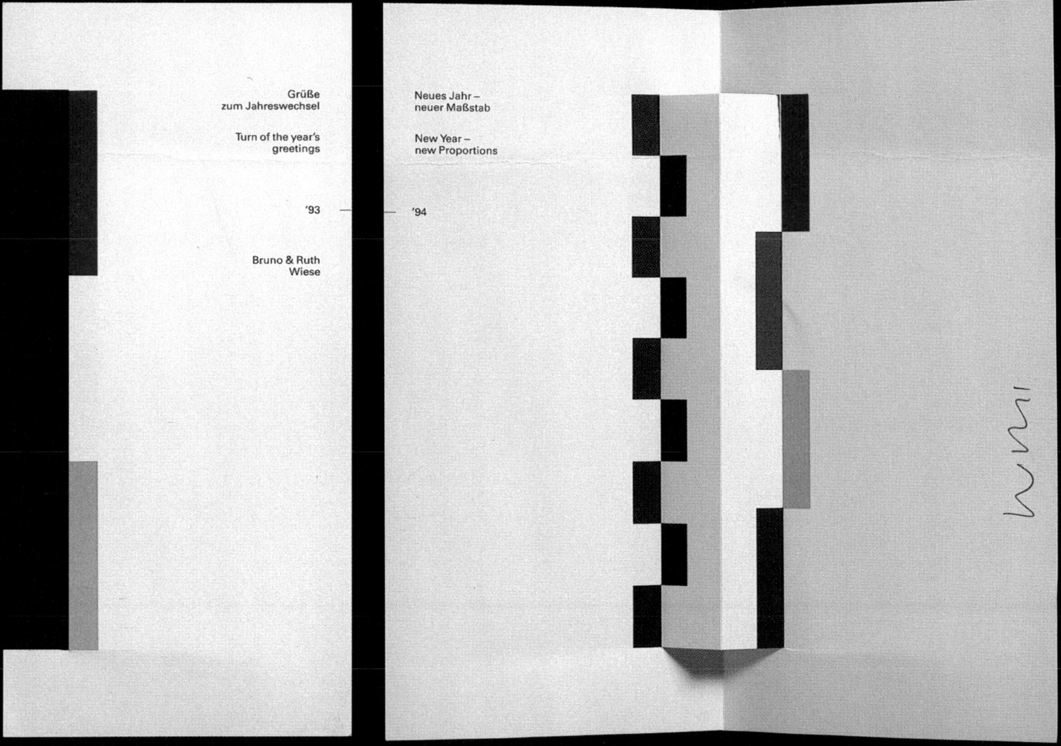

Grüße
zum Jahreswechsel

Turn of the year's
greetings

Neues Jahr –
neuer Maßstab

New Year –
new Proportions

'93 — '94

Bruno & Ruth
Wiese

1991
199209
1993a
1994четыре!

девяносто
четвертый

1994цифра

абвгдеёж
йклмнопр
уфхцчшщэ

(ABOVE) ART DIRECTOR: KEITH STEIMEL DESIGNER: CORNERSTONE STAFF AGENCY/CLIENT: CORNERSTONE DESIGN
ASSOCIATES COUNTRY: USA ◻ (OPPOSITE) ART DIRECTOR: BYRON JACOBS DESIGNERS: BYRON JACOBS, TRACY HOI
ILLUSTRATOR: PPA DESIGN LIMITED AGENCY: PPA DESIGN LIMITED CLIENT: GOLDEN HARVEST FILMS COUNTRY: HONG KONG

1991

1992

Golden Harvest

SAFETY FILM

EASTMAN 18 '1+1' LPP

Victor Dog

The symbol for quality
sounds today, and ever since
he first appeared in 1927 as
the symbol for RCA Victor.

1927년 처음 상표로 등장하여
지금까지 음의 명사를 뜻하는
명견

MUSEUM DOG

A true masterpiece
displaying extraordinary
artistic skill, depicting in
relief the wild dog of
Korea's Chosun Period
(1392-1910)

우리나라 조선시대의 명견으로
동방문헌이나 구도, 묘사면에서
매우 뛰어난 솜씨를 보여준 명견

FLANDERS DOG

Loving name given to
Patrasche, the local friend to
a poor youth who dreams of
becoming an artist.

화가를 꿈꾸는 가난한 소년과
충실스러운 개 파트라슈의
이야기에서

WINDSOR DOG

The eternally faithful canine
companion of the Duke of
Windsor, who gave up the
throne in the name of love.

사랑을 위해 왕관을 버린 윈저공의
영원한 충견

MOVIE DOG

A Hollywood super dog
Lassie, a well-known movie
star loved by millions.

영화로 유명으로 사랑을 받았던
영화주 견공 - 할리우드 명견
래시

(ALL IMAGES THIS SPREAD) ART DIRECTOR: DOO H. KIM DESIGNERS: DONGIL LEE, JIWON SHIN,
SEUNG HEE LEE AGENCY: DOOKIM DESIGN CLIENT: DOOKIM DESIGN COUNTRY: SOUTH KOREA

(OPPOSITE) ART DIRECTOR/DESIGNER/PHOTOGRAPHER: JEAN-BENOÎT LÉVY AGENCY/CLIENT: AND (TRAFIC GRAFIC) COUNTRY: SWITZERLAND

□ (ABOVE) DESIGNERS: KARIN MEYER, UTE WIEMER COPYWRITER: ROLF TAMMEN AGENCY/CLIENT: TAMMEN GMBH COUNTRY: GERMANY

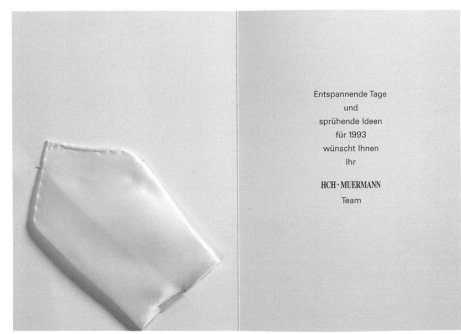

Entspannende Tage
und
sprühende Ideen
für 1993
wünscht Ihnen
Ihr

HCH · MUERMANN

Team

(This Page) Art Director: ROLAND SCHNEIDER Designer: MICHAELA BAUER Agency: BAUERS BÜRO Client: HCH. MUERMANN GMBH & CO. KG Country: GERMANY □ (Opposite Page) Art Director: DOO H. KIM Designers: DONGIL LEE, JIWON SHIN Agency: DOOKIM DESIGN Client: DOOKIM DESIGN Country: SOUTH KOREA

Corporate Symbol | Grid System

MONKEY '92 CORPORATE DESIGN MANUAL

Signature & Color Scheme | Incorrected Symbol

MONKEY'92

Monkey Red
Monkey Grey

MONKEY'92

MONKEY'92

MONKEY'92

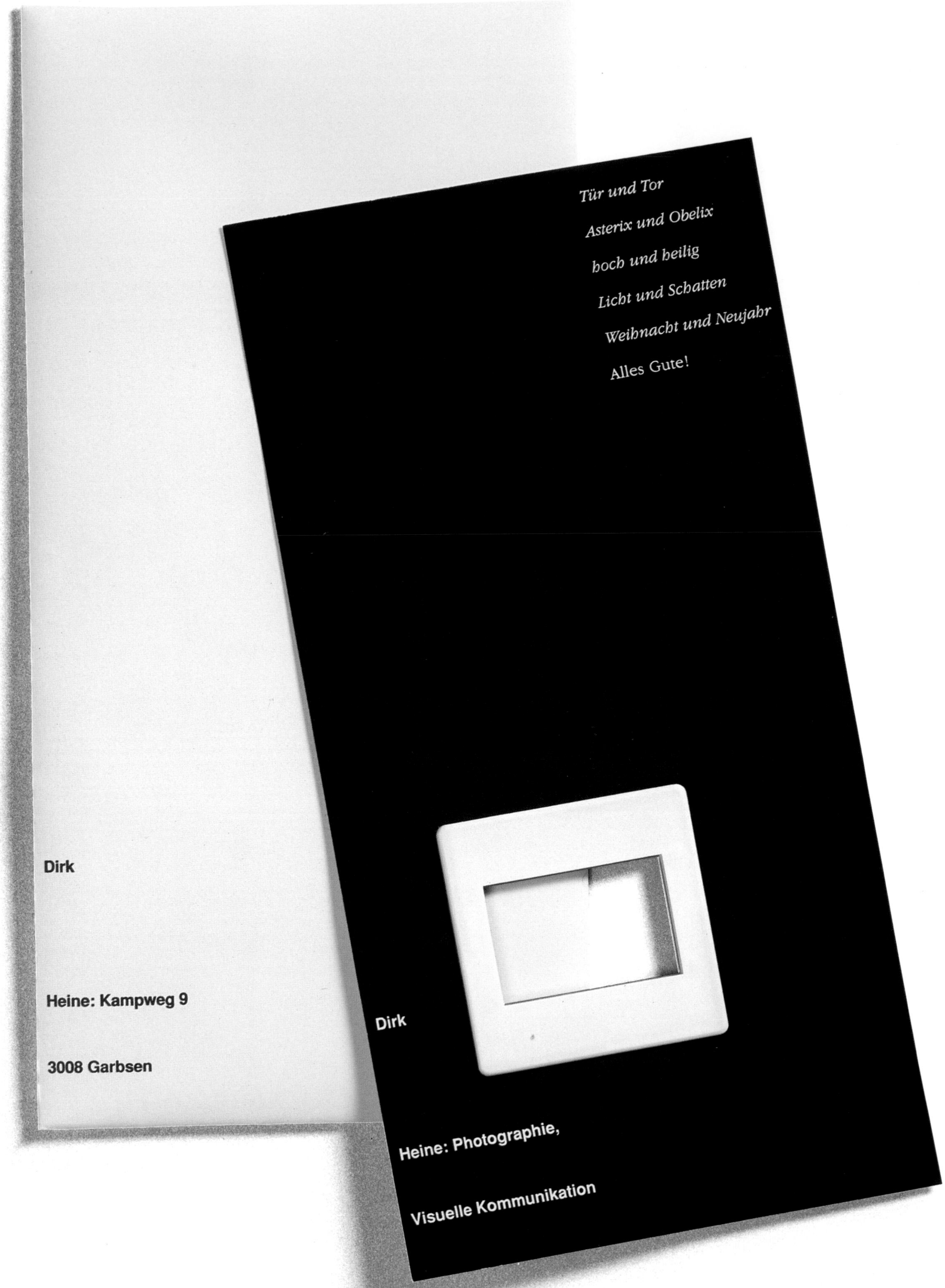

Tür und Tor

Asterix und Obelix

hoch und heilig

Licht und Schatten

Weihnacht und Neujahr

Alles Gute!

Dirk

Heine: Kampweg 9

3008 Garbsen

Dirk

Heine: Photographie,

Visuelle Kommunikation

(OPPOSITE) ART DIRECTOR/DESIGNER/CLIENT: DIRK HEINE COUNTRY: GERMANY □ (ABOVE) ART DIRECTOR/DESIGNER: MONICA
HEYMANN PHOTOGRAPHER: BRUNO AGENCY: RAIN MAKER ADVERTISING CLIENT: BRUNO PHOTOGRAPHY INC. COUNTRY: USA

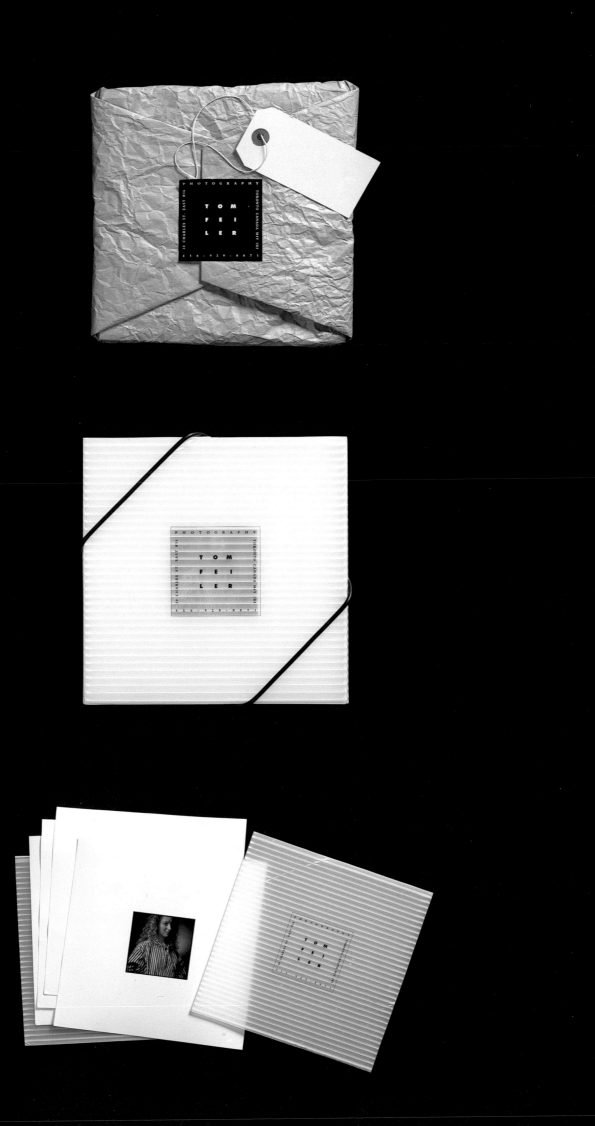

(OPPOSITE PAGE) ART DIRECTOR: MERCEDES ROTHWELL DESIGNER: MERCEDES ROTHWELL PHOTOGRAPHER: TOM FEILER
AGENCY: HAMBLY & WOOLLEY INC. CLIENT: TOM FEILER PHOTOGRAPHY COUNTRY: CANADA □ (THIS PAGE) ART
DIRECTOR/DESIGNER/COPYWRITER: NEAL ASHBY PHOTOGRAPHER/CLIENT: BARRY MYERS AGENCY: ASHBY DESIGN COUNTRY: USA

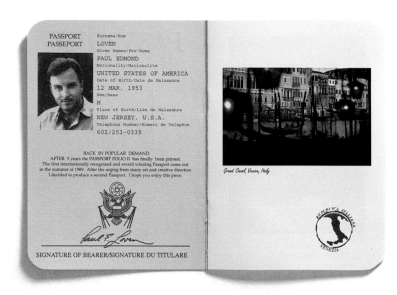

(OPPOSITE) PHOTOGRAPHER/CLIENT: WERNER GRITZBACH COUNTRY: GERMANY □ (ABOVE) ART DIRECTOR: RANDY PALMER
DESIGNERS: RON LELAND, PAUL LOVEN PHOTOGRAPHER: PAUL LOVEN CLIENT: PAUL LOVEN PHOTOGRAPHY, INC. COUNTRY: USA

(ABOVE) DESIGNER: ANDREW HOYNE PHOTOGRAPHER: ROB BLACKBURN AGENCY: ANDREW HOYNE
DESIGN CLIENT: SUN STUDIO COUNTRY: AUSTRALIA ☐ (OPPOSITE) ART DIRECTOR/PHOTOG-
RAPHER/CLIENT: COLIN GRAY DESIGNERS: COLIN GRAY, NICKY REGAN COUNTRY: GREAT BRITAIN

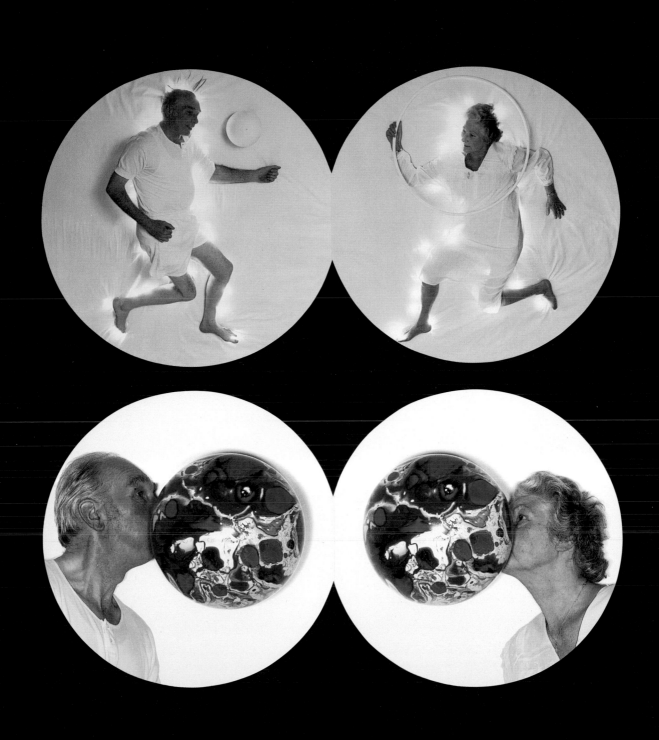

BURKE & FOSTER | PRINTING & COPYING

Menu
of Services

OPEN
24 hours

Nur öffnen, wenn Sie
was von Repro verstehen!

Aha! Sie sind also ein Reprofachmann!

Dann lassen Sie sich mal erzählen, was der
Biberle so macht.

Litho ...

Mit einem Gucker kann man zwar nur 12.56 mm²
eines Repros betrachten, ob allerdings eine
Qualitäts-Litho dahintersteckt, erkennt man bei
uns auf einen Blick.

Was sehen Sie unter der Lupe?

(OPPOSITE) ART DIRECTORS: BOB HAMBLY, BARBARA WOOLLEY, MERCEDES ROTHWELL DESIGNER: MERCEDES ROTHWELL
ILLUSTRATOR: SETH AGENCY: HAMBLY & WOOLLEY CLIENT: BURKE & FOSTER PRINTING & COPYING COUNTRY: CANADA
□ (ABOVE) ART DIRECTOR/DESIGNER/ILLUSTRATOR: WOLFGANG HASLINGER CLIENT: REPROTECHNIK BIBERLE COUNTRY: AUSTRIA

What a product. And what a forceful treatment of design elements to create the most compelling possible environment for the motivating components of the message.

What was human life compared to that? I almost felt sorry for Günter.

Almost. But I had no time for sentiment, anyway. I had a fight on my hands.

 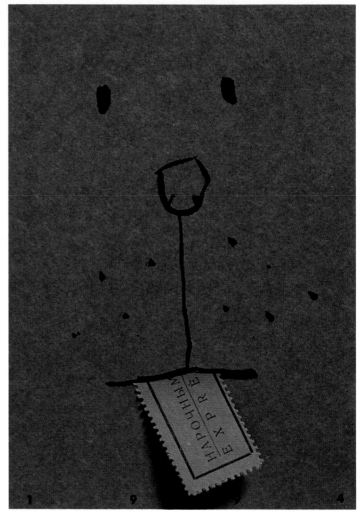

(ABOVE) ART DIRECTOR/DESIGNER/ILLUSTRATOR: ANDREY LOGVIN CLIENT: LINIA GRAFIC COUNTRY: RUSSIA □ (OPPOSITE) ART DIRECTOR: MAX LEY DESIGNERS: MAX LEY, GERD LANGKAFEL AGENCY: UNIVERS CLIENT: AGFA-COMPUGRAPHIC COUNTRY: GERMANY

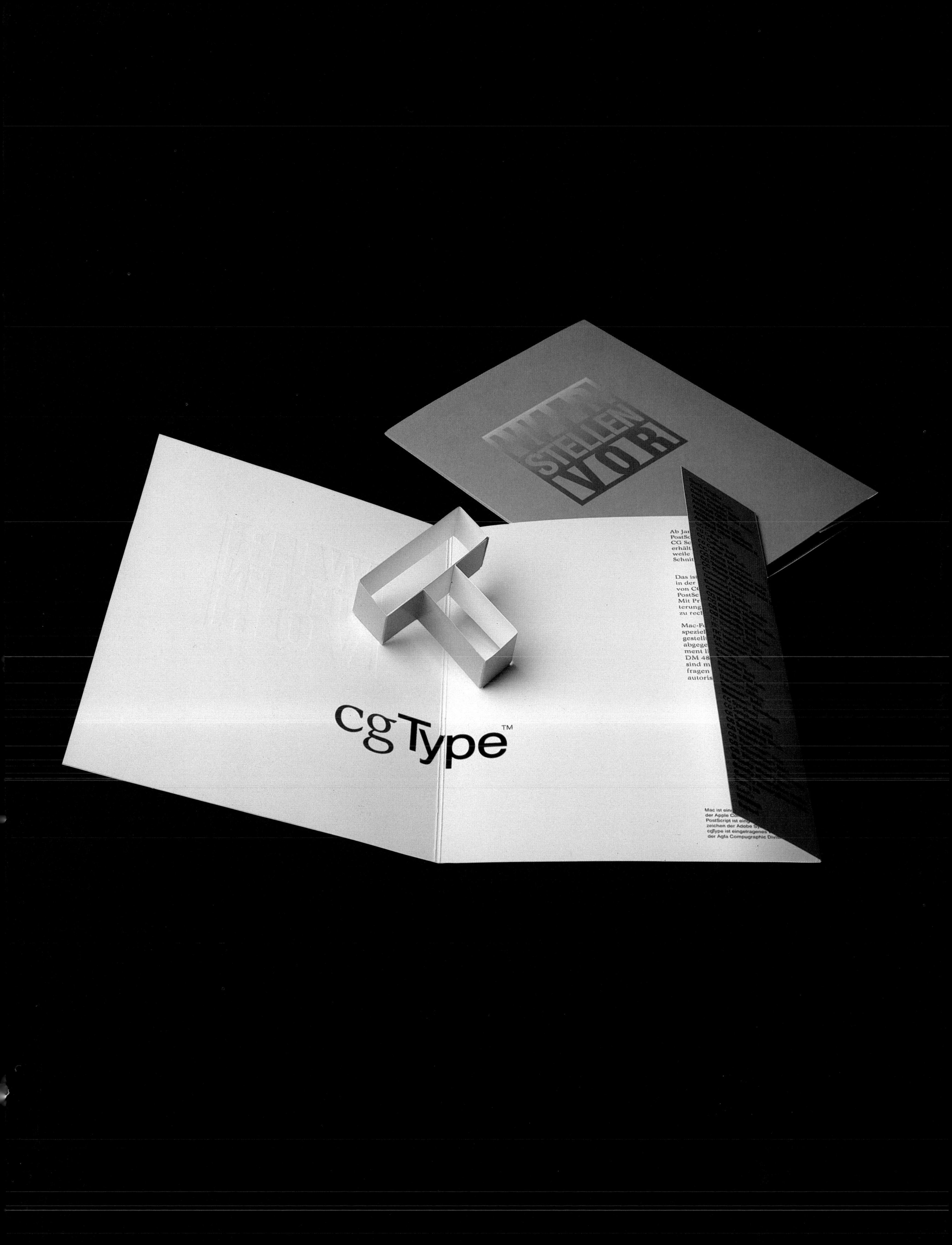

WIR
STELLEN
VOR

cgType™

Mac ist eine
der Apple Co
PostScript ist ein
zeichen der Adobe Sy
cgType ist eingetragenes
der Agfa Compugraphic Divisi

Ab Ja
PostSc
CG Sc
erhält
weile
Schnit

Das ist
in der
von CG
PostSc
Mit Pr
terung
zu rec

Mac-F
speziell
gestell
abgege
ment
DM 48
sind m
fragen
autoris

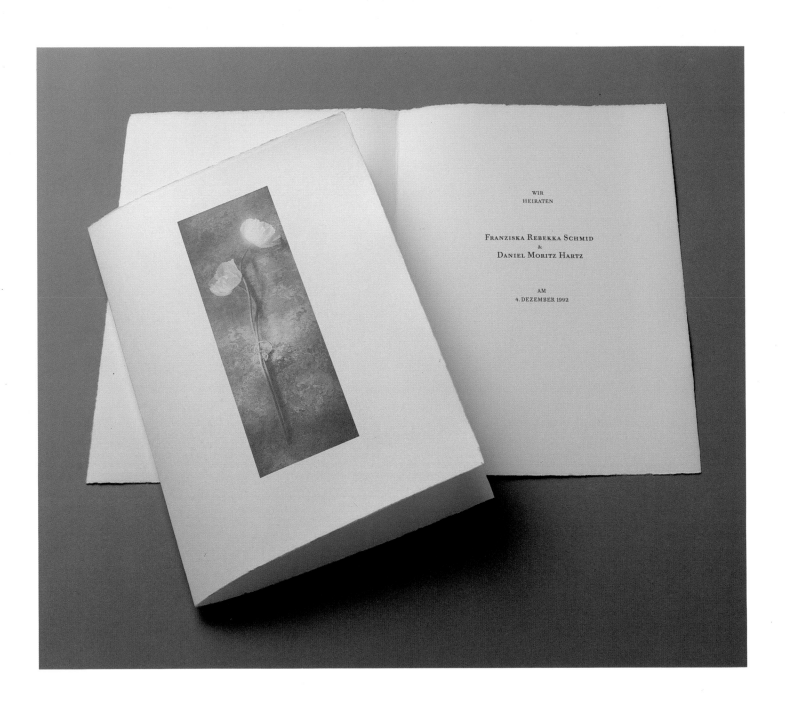

WIR
HEIRATEN

Franziska Rebekka Schmid
&
Daniel Moritz Hartz

AM
4. DEZEMBER 1992

(THIS PAGE) DESIGNER: FRANZISKA HARTZ PHOTOGRAPHER: DANIEL HARTZ COUNTRY: GERMANY □ (OPPOSITE PAGE)
ART WORKER: PAUL LEBER ILLUSTRATOR: PAUL LEBER PHOTOGRAPHER: HENRIETTE NIELSON COUNTRY: SWITZERLAND

TO ENTER DATA

Zajímá-li Vás, o co kráčí, zapište si do svých adresářů následující `TEL` adresy:
`VERONIKA MORAVCOVÁ` Famfulíkova 1133, 18200 Praha 8
`PAVEL LOUB` Kaňkovského 1239, 18200 Praha 8
a stiskněte `SET`.

TO SPECIFY TIME AND DATE

Co mají ti dva společného . . .?
`HOME` `FUNC` `FUNC` 1
11 `TIME/DATE` 00 `TIME/DATE`
9 `TIME/DATE` 10 `TIME/DATE`
1993 `TIME/DATE` `SET` aneb **9.10.1993 v 11** hodin.

TO USE THE FUNCTION KEY

Tiskněte `FUNC` tolikrát, kolikrát podle objevivších se neznámých slov uznáte za vhodné. Nedoporučuje se z rozmaru mačkat ALL DELETE, to jde všechno do háje.

TO SEARCH DATA

To není jen tak, zapsat si datum pro nic za nic. Pročež stiskněte `TEL` **Veronika Moravcová a Pavel Loub**
`SEARCH` `FUNC` `FUNC` 4 DATA COMM `4` 1 ONE ITEM
`1` SEARCH FOR? a víte totéž, co já, čili nic. Ale komu to jen trochu pálí , pochopí, že mají sňatbu, berou se aneb **stanou** se svými `ESC`.

TO ENTER THE SECRET AREA

heslo , ale je to marné, všichni se to dovědí.

INVITATION FROM

DESIGN © PAVEL BENEŠ, E.D.A., 1993 `SET`

(THIS PAGE) ART DIRECTOR/DESIGNER: PAVEL BENES AGENCY: GRAPHIC DESIGN PAVEL BENES COUNTRY: CZECH REPUBLIC ☐ (OPPOSITE PAGE) DESIGNER/ILLUSTRATOR: SASCHA WEIHS COUNTRY: GERMANY

ICH HABE DICH SO LIEB
ICH WÜRDE DIR OHNE BEDENKEN
EINE KACHEL AUS MEINEM OFEN
SCHENKEN.

ICH HABE DIR NICHTS GETAN.
NUN IST MIR TRAURIG ZU MUT.
AN DEN HÄNGEN DER EISENBAHN
LEUCHTET DER GINSTER SO GUT.

VORBEI — VERJÄHRT —
DOCH NIMMER VERGESSEN.
ICH REISE. -
ALLES, WAS LANGE WÄHRT,
IST LEISE.

DIE ZEIT ENTSTELLT
ALLE LEBEWESEN.
EIN HUND BELLT.
ER KANN NICHT LESEN.
ER KANN NICHT SCHREIBEN.
WIR KÖNNEN NICHT BLEIBEN.

ICH LACHE.
LÖCHER SIND DIE HAUPTSACHE
AN EINEM SIEB.

ICH HABE DICH SO LIEB!

...HEIRATEN AM
7. AUGUST 1993. ZU UNSERER
KIRCHLICHEN TRAUUNG UM
13.00 UHR
IN DER
KATHOLISCHEN KIRCHE
GUNDERSHOFEN LADEN WIR
RECHT HERZLICH EIN.
ANSCHLIESSEND FEIERN WIR
IN DER
LIXGASTSTÄTTE
IN BLAUSTEIN.
WIR FREUEN
UNS SEHR AUF EUCH!

BETTINA UND GERD

Bettina

PS.: ÜBER EINE
ZUSAGE BIS ZUM 27.6.1993
WÜRDEN WIR
UNS FREUEN!
TELEFON 07304/42483

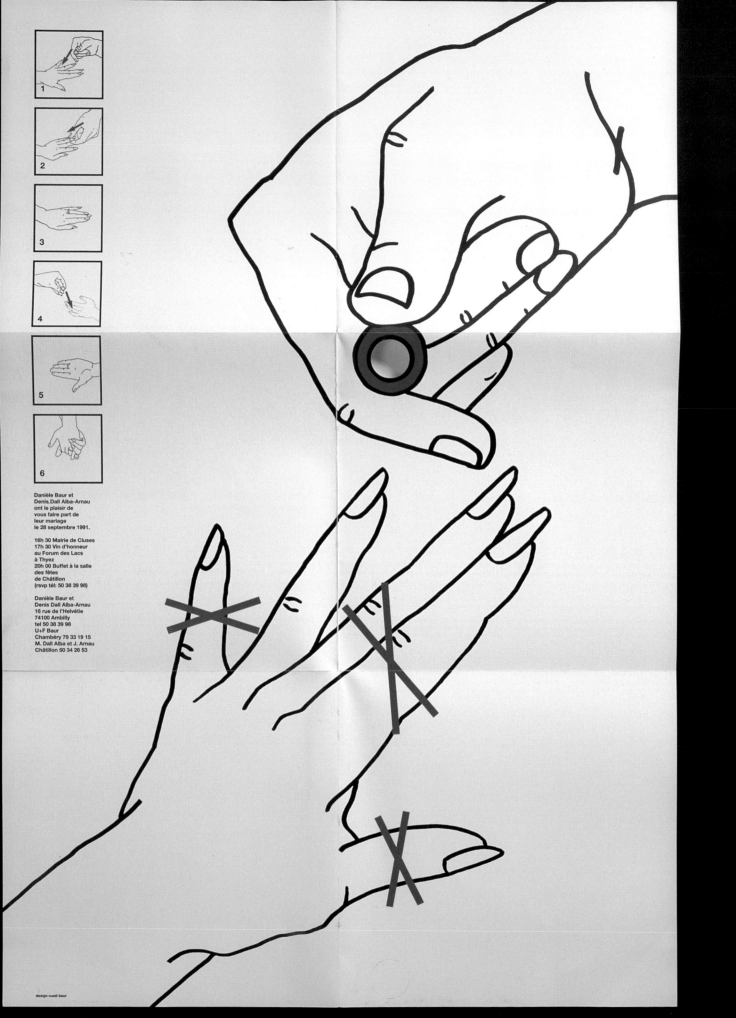

(OPPOSITE) DESIGNER: RUEDI BAUR AGENCY: INTÉGRAL RUEDI BAUR ET ASSOCIÉS COUNTRY: FRANCE □ (ABOVE) ART DIRECTOR/

DESIGNER/ILLUSTRATOR: JOEL TEMPLIN PHOTOGRAPHER: PAUL SINKLER AGENCY: CHARLES S. ANDERSON DESIGN COUNTRY: USA

 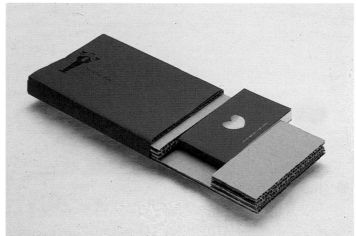

(THIS PAGE) ART DIRECTOR: MASAYUKI SHIMIZU DESIGNERS: MASAYUKI SHIMIZU, NIO KIMURA AGENCY: HETER·O·
DOXY PROTPRAST COUNTRY: JAPAN □ (OPPOSITE PAGE) ART DIRECTORS: WILLIE BARONET, STEVE GIBBS
DESIGNERS: WILLIE BARONET, KELLYE KIMBALL, BILL VANCE AGENCY: GIBBS BARONET COUNTRY: USA

ABC
DEFGHI
OPQRSTUVWXYZ

Ron Kostelny and Sheila Baldwin
were married in Dallas
Saturday March 14, 1992 at Holy
Cross Lutheran Church
The Kostelnys are residing at
3795 Vinecrest, Dallas,
Texas 75229, enjoying a relationship
that is letter perfect
No gifts, please

BRUCE HOLDEMAN
AND
MELODY BIGGS
WILL BE MARRIED
ON
SATURDAY,
NOVEMBER 20TH
AT 1:30 PM
AT
FIRST MENNONITE
CHURCH
430 WEST NINTH
AVENUE

COME CELEBRATE
WITH US!

RECEPTION
TO FOLLOW AT
TOURNAMENTS
6075 PARKWAY
DRIVE

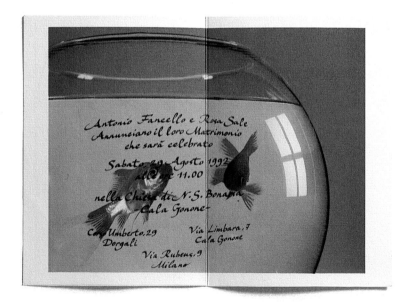

(OPPOSITE TOP AND CENTER) ART DIRECTOR/DESIGNER: BRUCE HOLDEMAN AGENCY: 601 DESIGN, INC. COUNTRY: USA □ (OPPOSITE BOTTOM) DESIGNER: LUCA VARASCHINI PHOTOGRAPHER: ANTONIO FANCELLO CLIENT: ANTONIO FANCELLO CALLIGRAPHY: ANNA RONCHI COUNTRY: ITALY □ (THIS PAGE) ART DIRECTOR/DESIGNER: WOLFGANG HASLINGER COUNTRY: AUSTRIA

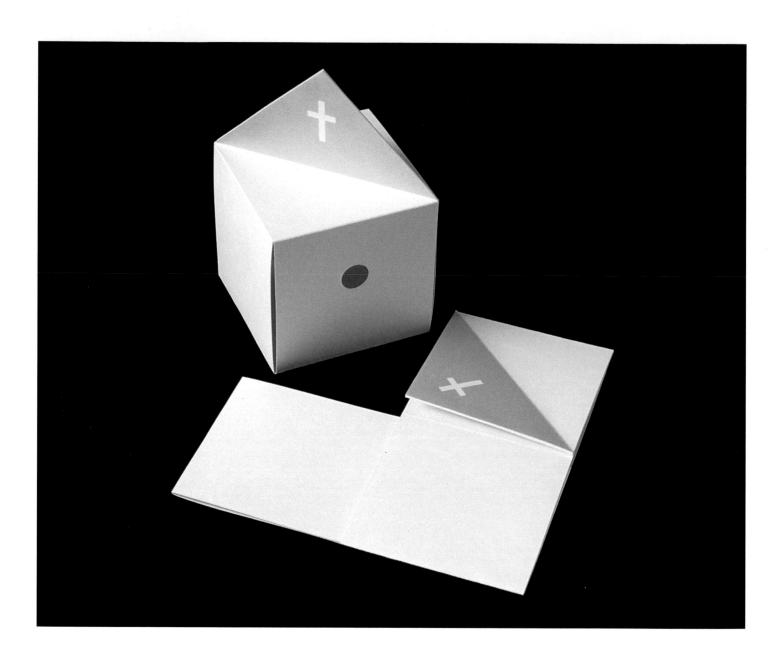

(ABOVE) ART DIRECTOR/DESIGNER: KEISUKE UNOSAWA ILLUSTRATOR: KEISUKE UNOSAWA AGENCY: KESIUKE UNOSAWA DESIGN
COUNTRY: JAPAN □ (OPPOSITE) ART DIRECTOR: ROSE DENDY YOUNG DESIGNER: CAROL DUFFETT COUNTRY: SOUTH AFRICA

קול ששון וקול שמחה ✡ קול חתן וקול כלה

Aaron and Adèle Searll
take great pleasure in inviting you to share
in the celebration of the marriage of their daughter
Catherine Jane
to
Stephen John
son of Jack Abraham & the late Jennifer Abraham
on Sunday 10 April 1994 at
the Gardens Synagogue, Hatfield Street, Cape Town
at 6.30 pm
to be followed by a Dinner Dance
at Monterey, 12-14 Klaassens Road, Bishopscourt.

RSVP: Linda Lee 761-8000 before 18 March 1994
Dress: Black Tie

(ABOVE) DESIGNER: NINA ULMAJA AGENCY: NINA ULMAJA GRAFISK FORM COUNTRY: SWEDEN □ (OPPOSITE) ART DIRECTOR: PAT GORMAN
DESIGNERS: PAT GORMAN, TUNA FLORES ILLUSTRATOR/COPYWRITER: LINDA BARRY AGENCY: PAT GORMAN DESIGN COUNTRY: USA

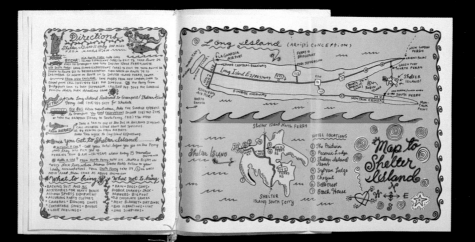

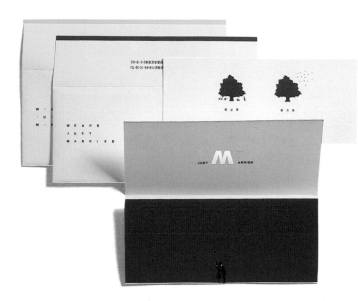

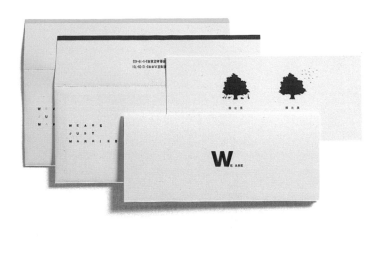

(ABOVE) ART DIRECTOR/DESIGNER: KEISUKE UNOSAWA AGENCY: KEISUKE UNOSAWA DESIGN COUNTRY: JAPAN □ (BOTTOM) DESIGNER/
ILLUSTRATOR: SASCHA WEIHS COUNTRY: GERMANY □ (OPPOSITE TOP) ART DIRECTOR/DESIGNER/COPYWRITER/AGENCY: ROY
CARRUTHERS COUNTRY: USA □ (BOTTOM) ART DIRECTORS/DESIGNERS: GREG MORGAN, CANDACE BUCHANAN COUNTRY: USA

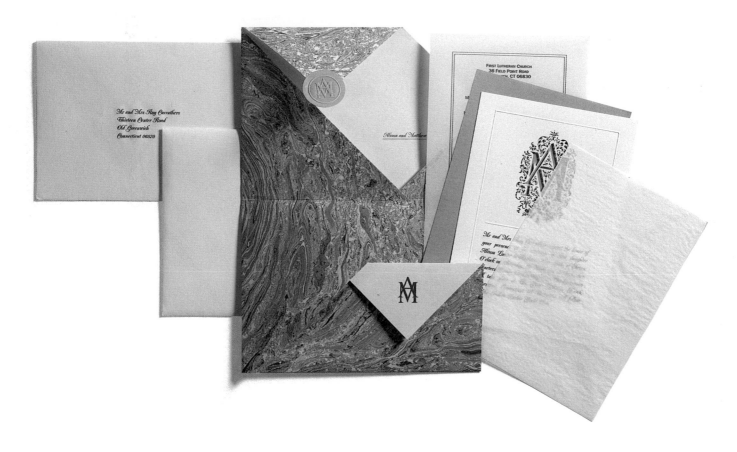

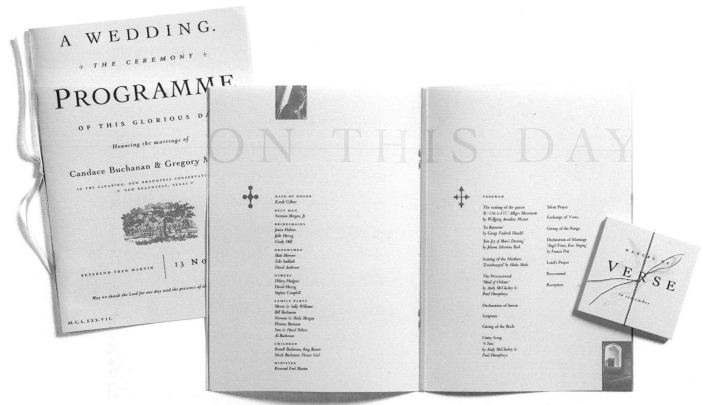

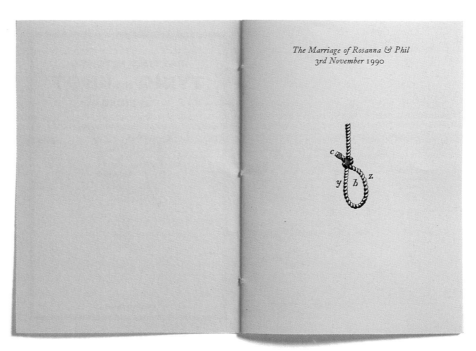

Margit Drexel

Moosmahdstr. 8, A-6850 Dornbirn

Josef Horber

Steinwichslen 20, CH-9052 Niederteufen

Gottesdienst

Kapelle Eichenwis/Oberriet SG

Samstag, 10. Dezember 1988, 15.30 Uhr

Hochzeitsfeier

Hotel Messmer, Kornmarkt 16

A-6901 Bregenz, 18.30 Uhr.

Margit Drexel

Moosmahdstr. 8, A-6850 Dornbirn

Josef Horber

Steinwichslen 20, CH-9052 Niederteufen

Gottesdienst

Kapelle Eichenwis/Oberriet SG

Samstag, 10. Dezember 1988, 15.30 Uhr

Hochzeitsfeier

Hotel Messmer, Kornmarkt 16

A-6901 Bregenz, 18.30 Uhr.

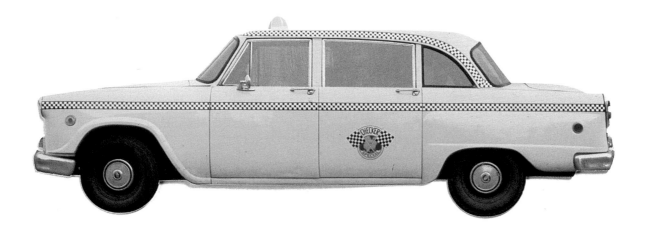

(THIS SPREAD) ART DIRECTOR/DESIGNER/ILLUSTRATOR: JEFFREY MILSTEIN CLIENT: PAPER HOUSE PRODUCTIONS COUNTRY: USA

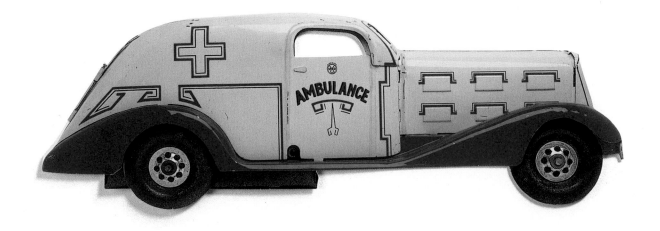

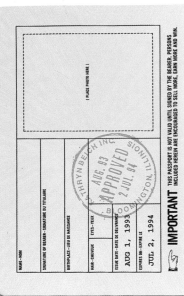
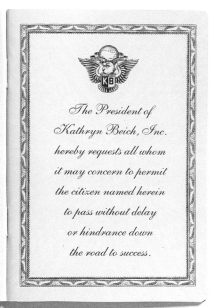

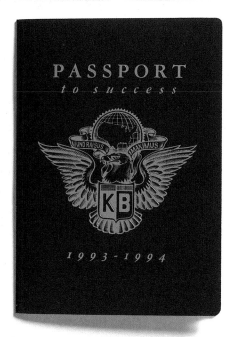

Grand Prize

If you earn the greatest number of miles during the course of the program (and your total net sales have increased over last year) you will receive this incredible prize.

DREAM VACATION

Imagine a five-day getaway to a luxurious resort in Arizona next winter. Or maybe a trip to Washington D.C. is more to your liking with historic monuments and fascinating museums. Of course if you want to breathe some clean mountain air you could head north for a five-day adventure in the Canadian Rockies. Perhaps you'd like to explore the world of fine dining during a five-night stay in San Francisco. How about a Caribbean cruise aboard the incredible Nordic Empress? You could even spend time south of the border on a fun in the sun trip to the sparkling beaches of Cancun, Mexico. These are just some examples of how you could spend your dream vacation fund – it's up to you to decide where and when you want to go!

20

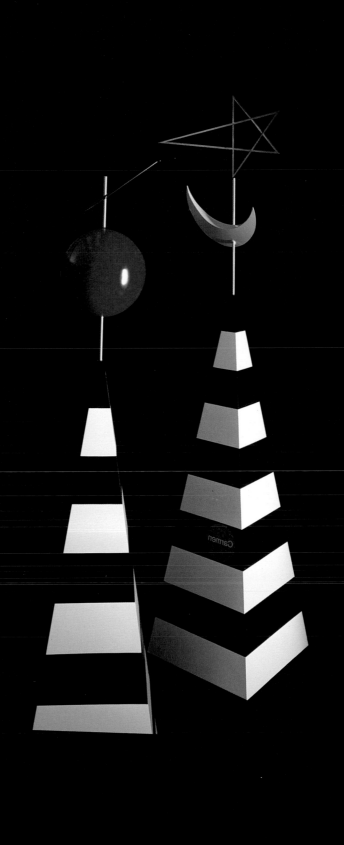

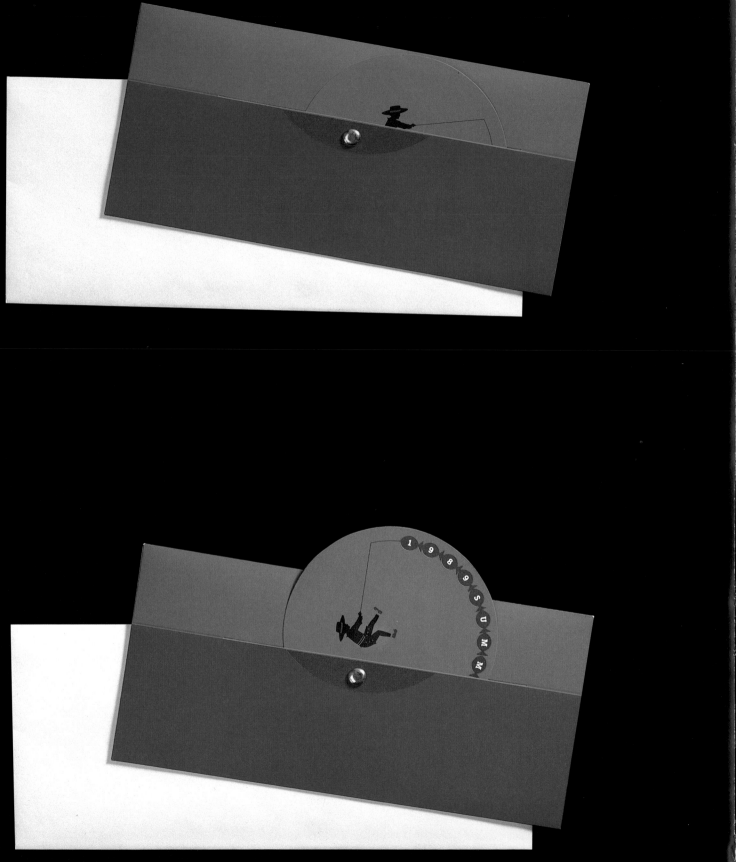

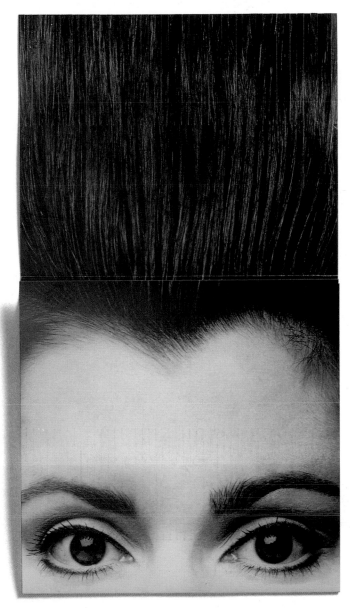

(PRECEDING SPREAD LEFT) ART DIRECTOR/DESIGNER: BRUCE EDWARDS ILLUSTRATOR: JAKE AGENCY: RAPP COLLINS COMMUNICATIONS CLIENT: KATHRYN BEICH (NESTLE-BEICH'S FUNDRAISING) COUNTRY: USA □ (PRECEDING SPREAD RIGHT) ART DIRECTOR: GARRY EMERY DESIGNER/AGENCY: EMERY VINCENT ASSOC. CLIENT: CARMEN FURNITURE (SALES) PTY LIMITED COUNTRY: AUSTRALIA □ (OPPOSITE PAGE) ART DIRECTOR/DESIGNER/ILLUSTRATOR: KEISUKE UNOSAWA AGENCY/CLIENT: KEISUKE UNO-SAWA DESIGN COUNTRY: JAPAN □ (THIS PAGE) ART DIRECTOR/DESIGNER: KEN HERNDON PHOTOG-RAPHER: JOSEPH HUMPHREY AGENCY: KEN HERNDON GRAPHIC DESIGN CLIENT: IMAGES HAIR SALON COUNTRY: USA

(ABOVE) ART DIRECTOR/DESIGNER: SCOTT MIRES PHOTOGRAPHER: CARL VANDERSCHUIT ILLUSTRATOR: TRACY SABIN AGENCY: MIRES DESIGN COUNTRY: USA □ (OPPOSITE) ART DIRECTOR/DESIGNER/ILLUSTRATOR/AGENCY: SHIGERU AKIZUKI COUNTRY: JAPAN

815, 4-27-32 IKEJIRI
SETAGAYA-KU TOKYO.
TEL·FAX(03) 412-1371
Shigeru Akizuki

862

熊本市西本町
8-1-7-25
岡部 敏様

〒154

815, 4-27-32 IKEJIRI
SETAGAYA-KU TOKYO.
TEL·FAX(03) 412-1371
Shigeru Akizuki

〒154

815, 4-27-32 IKEJIRI
SETAGAYA-KU TOKYO.
TEL·FAX(03) 412-1371
Shigeru Akizuki

〒154

815, 4-27-32 IKEJIRI
SETAGAYA-KU TOKYO.
TEL·FAX(03) 412-1371
Shigeru Akizuki

〒154

815, 4-27-32 IKEJIRI
SETAGAYA-KU TOKYO.
TEL·FAX(03) 412-1371
Shigeru Akizuki

〒154

815, 4-27-32 IKEJIRI
SETAGAYA-KU TOKYO.
TEL·FAX(03) 412-1371
Shigeru Akizuki

〒154

815, 4-27-32 IKEJIRI
SETAGAYA-KU TOKYO.
TEL·FAX(03) 412-1371
Shigeru Akizuki

〒154

815, 4-27-32 IKEJIRI
SETAGAYA-KU TOKYO.
TEL·FAX(03) 412-1371
Shigeru Akizuki

〒154

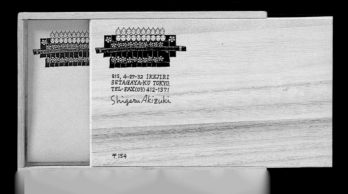

815, 4-27-32 IKEJIRI
SETAGAYA-KU TOKYO.
TEL·FAX(03) 412-1371
Shigeru Akizuki

〒154

815, 4-27-32 IKEJIRI
SETAGAYA-KU TOKYO.
TEL·FAX(03) 412-1371
Shigeru Akizuki

〒154

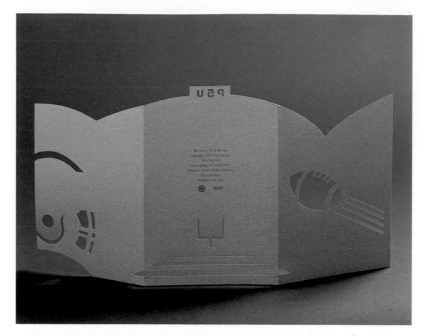

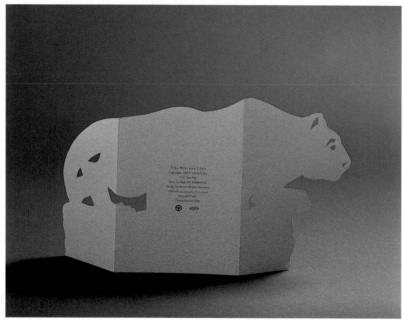

(OPPOSITE PAGE) ART DIRECTOR: KRISTIN SOMMESE DESIGNER: KRISTIN SOMMESE AGENCY: SOMMESE DESIGN CLIENT: CUTCARDS INC.
COUNTRY: USA □ (THIS PAGE) ART DIRECTOR/DESIGNER: XIAO YONG CLIENT: YÉ DESIGN COUNTRY: CHINA □ (FOLLOWING
PAGE) ART DIRECTOR: SEYMOUR CHWAST DESIGNER: SEYMOUR CHWAST ILLUSTRATORS: R. KENTON NELSON, ROBERT
CRAWFORD, LOU BEACH, DAVE JONASON DESIGN FIRM: THE PUSHPIN GROUP CLIENT: THE PUSHPIN ASSOCIATES
COUNTRY: USA □ (PAGE 224) ART DIRECTOR: ISABELLE PAQUIN DESIGNER: JEAN-FRANÇOIS COUVIGNOU ILLUSTRATOR:
FRÉDÉRIC EIBNER AGENCY: SUN COMMUNICATIONS DESIGN CLIENT: DOMTAR SPECIALTY FINE PAPERS COUNTRY: CANADA

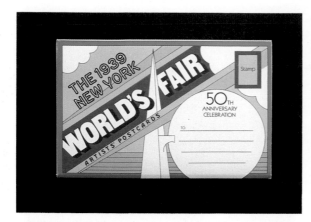

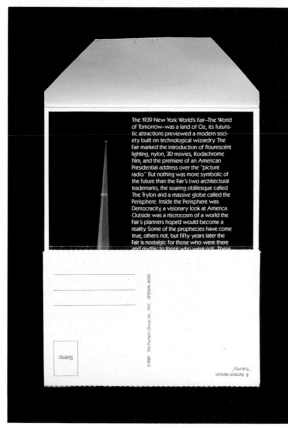

INDEX

VERZEICHNIS

INDEX

···

AGENCIES·STUDIOS

···

CALL FOR ENTRIES

EINLADUNG

APPEL D'ENVOIS

CALL FOR ENTRIES

Graphis Poster 96 · Entry Deadline: April 30, 1995

■ Advertising, cultural, and social posters. Eligibility: All work produced between May 1994 and April 1995. ● Plakate für Werbezwecke sowie kulturelle und soziale Plakate. In Frage kommen: Arbeiten, die zwischen Mai 1994 und April 1995 entstanden sind. ▲ Affiches publicitaires, culturelles et sociales. Seront admis: tous les travaux réalisés entre mai 1994 et avril 1995.

Graphis Photo 96 · Entry Deadline: August 31, 1995

■ Ads, catalogs, invitations, announcements, record covers, and calendars on any subject.. Photographs taken for consumer or trade magazines, newspapers, books and corporate publications. Personal studies on any subject. Experimental or student work on any subject. Eligibility: All work produced between September 1994 and August 1995. ● Anzeigen, Kataloge, Plattenhüllen, Kalender. Photos für Zeitschriften, Zeitungen, Bücher und Firmenpublikationen. Persönliche Studien. Experimentelle Aufnahmen oder Studentenarbeiten. In Frage kommen: Arbeiten, die zwischen September 1994 und August 1995 entstanden sind. ▲ Publicité, catalogues, invitations, annonces, pochettes de disques, calendriers. Reportages pour magazines et journaux, livres et publications d'entreprise. Études personnelles, créations expérimentales ou projets d'étudiants. Seront admis: tous les travaux réalisés entre septembre 1994 et août 1995.

Graphis Design 97 · Entry Deadline: November 30, 1995

■ Ads; promotion brochures, catalogs, invitations, record covers, announcements, logos, corporate campaigns, calendars, books, book covers, packaging, company magazines; newspapers, consumer or trade magazines, annual reports; illustration. Eligibility: All work produced between December 1, 1994 and November 30, 1995. ● Werbung, Broschüren, Kataloge, Plattenhüllen, Logos, Firmenkampagnen, Kalender, Bücher, Buchumschläge, Packungen. Zeitschriften, Hauszeitschriften, Jahresberichte, Illustrationen. In Frage kommen: Arbeiten, die zwischen Dezember 1994 und November 1995 entstanden sind. ▲ Publicité; brochures, catalogues, invitations, pochettes de disques, annonces, logos, identité visuelle, calendriers, livres, packaging;journaux, revues, magazines de sociétés, rapports annuels; illustration. Seront admis: les travaux réalisés entre décembre 1994 et novembre 1995.

■ **What to send:** Reproduction-quality duplicate transparencies (4x5" or 35mm). They are required for large, bulky or valuable pieces. ALL 35MM SLIDES MUST BE CARDBOARD-MOUNTED, NO GLASS SLIDE MOUNTS PLEASE! *Please mark the transparencies with your name.* If you do send printed pieces they should be unmounted, but well protected. WE REGRET THAT ENTRIES CANNOT BE RETURNED. ● **Was einsenden:** Wenn immer möglich, schicken Sie uns bitte reproduktionsfähige Duplikatdias. *Bitte Dias mit Ihrem Namen versehen.* Bitte schicken Sie auf keinen Fall Originaldias. KLEINBILDDIAS BITTE IM KARTONRAHMEN, KEIN GLAS! Falls Sie uns das gedruckte Beispiel schicken, bitten wir Sie, dieses gut geschützt aber nicht aufgezogen zu senden. WIR BEDAUERN, DASS EINSENDUNGEN NICHT ZURÜCKGESCHICKT WERDEN KÖNNEN. ■ **Que nous envoyer:** Nous vous recommandons de nous faire parvenir de préférence des duplicata de diapositives (4x5" ou 35mm. N'oubliez pas d'inscrire votre nom dessus). NE PAS ENVOYER DE DIAPOSITIVES SOUS VERRE! Si vous désirez envoyer des travaux imprimés, protégez-les, mais ne les montez pas sur carton. *Nous vous signalons que les envois que vous nous aurez fait parvenir ne pourront vous être retournés.*

■ **How to package your entry:** Please tape (do not glue) the completed entry form (or a copy) to the back of each piece. Please do not send anything by air freight. Write "No Commercial Value" on the package, and label it "Art for Contest." ● **Wie und wohin senden:** Bitte befestigen Sie das ausgefüllte Einsendeetikett (oder eine Kopie davon) mit Klebstreifen (nicht kleben) auf jeder Arbeit und legen Sie noch ein Doppel davon lose bei. Bitte auf keinen Fall Luft- oder Bahnfracht senden. Deklarieren Sie «Ohne jeden Handelswert» und «Arbeitsproben für Wettbewerb». ▲ **Comment préparer votre envoi:** Veuillez scotcher (ne pas coller) au dos de chaque spécimen les étiquettes dûment remplies. Nous vous prions également de faire un double de chaque étiquette, que vous joindrez à votre envoi, mais sans le coller ou le fixer. Ne nous expédiez rien en fret aérien. Indiquez «Sans aucune valeur commerciale» et «Echantillons pour concours».

■ **Entry fees** Single entries: United States U.S. $20; Germany, DM 20,00; all other countries, SFr 20.00. Campaigns or series of three or more pieces: North America, U.S. $50, Germany DM 50,00, All other countries SFr 50.00. These entry fees do not apply to countries with exchange controls or to students (please send copy of student identification). ● **Einsendegebühren:** Für jede einzelne Arbeit: Deutschland DM 20.00, alle andern Länder SFr 20.00. Für jede Kampagne oder Serie von drei oder mehr Stück: Deutschland DM 50.00, übrige Länder SFr 50.00. Für Studenten (Ausweiskopie mitschicken) und Länder mit Devisenbeschränkugen gelten diese Einsendegebühren nicht. ▲ **Droits d'admission**: Envoi d'un seul travail: pour l'Amérique du Nord, US$ 20.00; pour tous les autres pays: SFr. 20.00. Campagne ou série de trois travaux ou plus pour un seul concours: Amérique du Nord, US$ 50.00; autres pays: SFr. 50.00. Les participants de pays qui connaissent des restrictions monétaires sont dispensés des droits d'admission, au même titre que les étudiants (veuillez envoyer une photocopie de la carte d'étudiant).

■ **Where to send:** Entries from the United States and Canada should be sent to the New York office and checks should be made payable to GRAPHIS US, INC, NEW YORK. Entries from all other countries should be sent to the Zurich office and checks should be made payable to GRAPHIS PRESS CORP., ZURICH. ● **Wohin senden:** Bitte senden Sie uns Ihre Arbeiten an Graphis Zürich zusammen mit einem Scheck, ausgestellt in SFr. (auf eine Schweizer Bank ziehen oder Eurocheck) oder überweisen Sie den Betrag auf PC Luzern 60-3520-6 oder PSchK Frankfurt 3000 57-602 (BLZ 50010060). ▲ **Où envoyer:** Veuillez envoyer vos travaux à Graphis Zurich et joindre un'chèque tiré sur une banque suisse ou un Eurochèque; ou verser le montant sur le compte chèque postal Lucerne 60–3520–6.

Graphis Press, Dufourstrasse 107, CH-8008 Zürich, Switzerland, telephone: 41-1-383 82 11, fax: 41-1-383 16 43
Graphis US, Inc., 141 Lexington Avenue, New York, NY 10016, telephone: (212) 532 9387, fax: (212) 213 3229

E N T R Y   F O R M

I wish to enter the attached in the following Graphis competition:

☐ **GRAPHIS POSTER 96** (DEADLINE APRIL 30, 1995)
CATEGORY CODES/KATEGORIEN/CATÉGORIES
☐ **PO1**   ADVERTISING/WERBUNG/PUBLICITÉ
☐ **PO2**   PROMOTION
☐ **PO3**   CULTURE/KULTUR
☐ **PO4**   SOCIAL/GESELLSCHAFT/SOCIÉTÉ

☐ **GRAPHIS PHOTO 96** (DEADLINE AUGUST 31, 1995)
CATEGORY CODES/KATEGORIEN/CATÉGORIES
☐ **PH1**   FASHION/MODE
☐ **PH2**   JOURNALISM/JOURNALISMUS
☐ **PH3**   STILL LIFE/STILLEBEN/NATURE MORTE
☐ **PH4**   FOOD/LEBENSMITTEL/CUISINE
☐ **PH5**   PEOPLE/MENSCHEN/PERSONNES
☐ **PH6**   PRODUCTS/PRODUKTE/PRODUITS
☐ **PH7**   LANDSCAPES/LANDSCHAFTEN/EXTÉRIEURS
☐ **PH8**   ARCHITECTURE/ARCHITEKTUR
☐ **PH9**   WILD LIFE/TIERE/ANIMAUX
☐ **PH10** SPORTS/SPORT
☐ **PH11** FINE ART/KUNST/ART

☐ **GRAPHIS DESIGN 97** (DEADLINE NOVEMBER 30, 1995)
CATEGORY CODES/KATEGORIEN/CATÉGORIES
☐ **DE1**   ADVERTISING/WERBUNG/ PUBLICITÉ
☐ **DE2**   BOOKS/BÜCHER/LIVRES
☐ **DE3**   BROCHURES/BROSCHÜREN
☐ **DE4**   CALENDARS/KALENDER/CALENDRIERS
☐ **DE5**   CORPORATE IDENTITY
☐ **DE6**   EDITORIAL/REDAKTIONELL/RÉDACTIONNEL
☐ **DE7**   ILLUSTRATION
☐ **DE8**   PACKAGING/VERPACKUNG
☐ **DE9**   MISCELLANEOUS/ANDERE/DIVERS

I HEREBY GRANT PERMISSION FOR THE ATTACHED MATERIAL TO BE PUBLISHED FREE OF CHARGE IN ANY GRAPHIS BOOK, ANY ARTICLE IN GRAPHIS MAGAZINE, OR ANY ADVERTISEMENT, BROCHURE OR OTHER MATERIAL PRODUCED FOR THE PURPOSE OF PROMOTING GRAPHIS PUBLICATIONS. I AGREE THAT THE PHONE NUMBERS OF THE CREATIVE PERSONNEL AFFILIATED WITH SELECTED ENTRIES MAY BE ENTERED IN THE INDEX OF THE BOOK.

SIGNATURE:

SENDER:
COMPANY, ADDRESS

TELEPHONE   FAX
ART DIRECTOR:
ADDRESS

TELEPHONE   FAX
DESIGNER:
ADDRESS

TELEPHONE   FAX
PHOTOGRAPHER:
ADDRESS

TELEPHONE   FAX
ILLUSTRATOR:
ADDRESS

TELEPHONE   FAX
AGENCY, STUDIO:
ADDRESS

TELEPHONE   FAX
CLIENT:
ADDRESS

G R A P H I S   B O O K S

GRAPHIS MAGAZINE

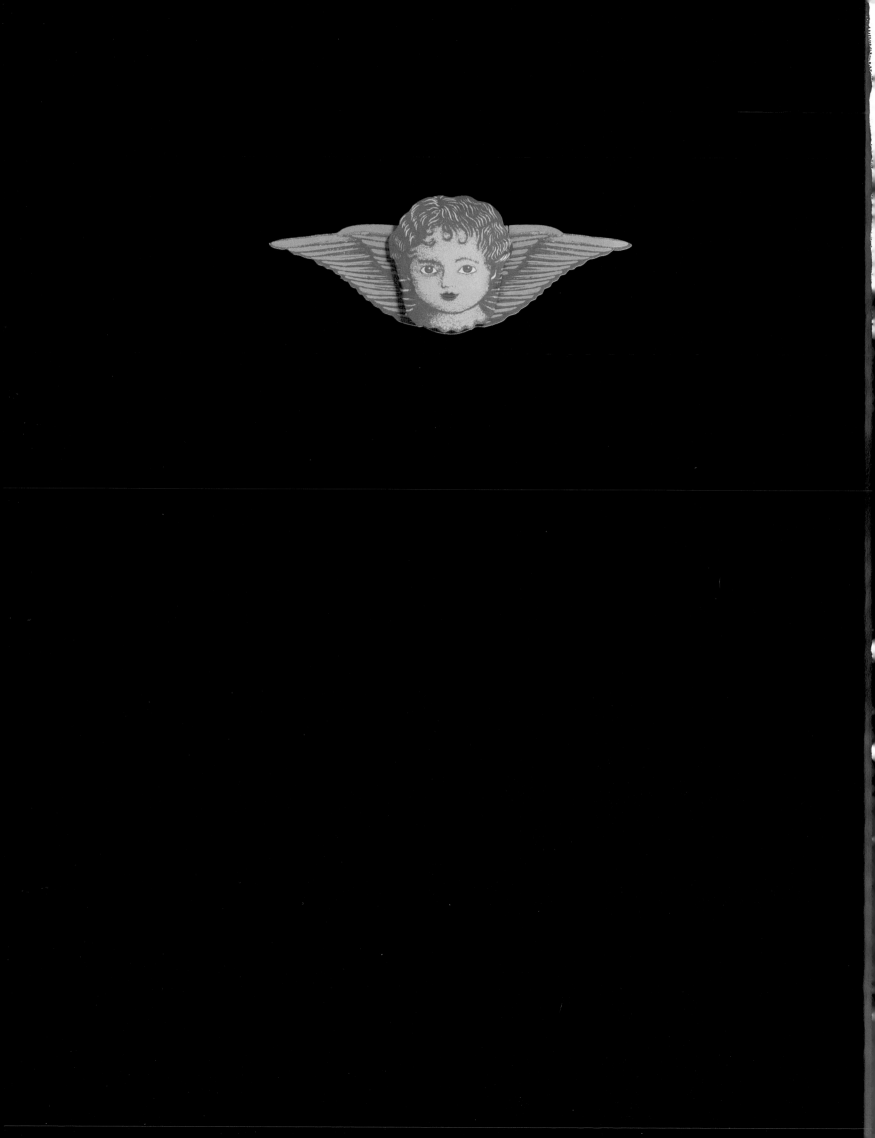